# CALLING THE CALLED

## A CALL TO SAVE AMERICA

Dennis P. Delisle
P.O. Box 1475
Morgan Hill, Ca. 95038
Email: dennis@
callingthecalled.com

PRAYERS FOR OUR COUNTRY

FOR WHEN THE RIGHTEOUS ARE IN AUTHORITY, THE
PEOPLE REJOICE, IN JESUS NAME!
PROVERBS 29:2

THE LORD IS ON MY SIDE; I SHALL NOT FEAR.
PSALM 118:6

TODAY I GIVE THANKS FOR OUR COUNTRY AND ITS
GOVERNMENT. I UPHOLD OUR LEADERS IN PRAYER
BEFORE YOU.
1 TIMOTHY 2:1

WE PRAY THEY HAVE WISDOM, DISCERNMENT AND
KNOWLEDGE FOR EVERY DECISION THEY MAKE.
PROVERBS 2:6

POUR OUT YOUR SPIRIT UPON THEM AND MAKE YOUR
WORD KNOWN TO THEM.
PROVERBS 1:23

*Prayers from Rhemarx –
www.clingtoyourconfession.com

SPECIAL ACKNOWLEDGEMENT AND A SPECIAL THANK
YOU TO THE
CONTRIBUTING WRITERS:


RON BALL

NEIL MAMMEN

BOB MCEWEN


A SPECIAL THANK YOU TO MY WIFE SHARON WHO
SUPPORTS ME IN ALL MY ENDEAVORS.

TO MY PARENTS FRANK & RITA DELISLE WHO HAVE SET
THE EXAMPLES THAT HAVE MOLDED MY LIFE.

THANKS TO MY WIFE SHARON AND MY DAUGHTER
ANNETTE DELISLE FOR EDITING AND REVISIONS.

# TABLE OF CONTENTS

# CHAPTER 1 – WHY THIS BOOK?

In your gut you know that there is something seriously wrong with our country today. We are heading in a direction that most of us would consider a nightmare, yet we don't know how to wake up. This book will help you to take action in the areas that God has placed you. The days of saying "it's someone else's problem" are over. It's our problem for those who believe in the faith that inspired our country's birth and the people who sacrificed so much to create it. The challenge is not the Constitution; it is the people that are elected to protect the constitution. Many Christians today elect people to office that they have no idea of what principles guide them in their decision making process. Today what politicians say is not what they do in many cases. You have to know their voting record to really understand what they stand for. This takes time and energy. The challenge is that we get busy making a living, trying to live up to our spiritual duties and taking care of our families. In many cases we leave the election of those who make the laws that govern our lives up to other people. The challenge is that when we elect people that do not share the same principles that are expressed in the Bible, we have a major conflict. I have heard it said that only 5% of the people in Germany were Nazis in the 1930's that lead to World War II. It is also stated that only about 20% of the British citizens in the colonies of America stood up to declare their freedom from Great Britain. Today it looks like somewhere between 5% and 20% of the people in the United States are moving America away from Godly principles to secularism. The 80% to 95% can't remain uninvolved and uneducated any more if we are to save the principles of the Founders established for our country.

People in America who believe in Allah, Mohammad, Buddha, or are Atheists need to be tolerant of Christian principles. Why? Because the United States of America was founded on these Judeo-Christian principles. As much as revisionists have tried to eliminate this influence from our history books, the U.S. congressional records of the actual writings of the Founding Fathers proves beyond any reasonable doubt that one of the major influences in the writing of our Constitution was the Bible.

Christians should be tired of being pushed around and made fun of for their faith. We have to stand up for our heritage and make elected officials more afraid of how the Jews and Christians vote than the ACLU (American Civil Liberties Union), GLAAD (Gay & Lesbian Alliance Against Defamation), Atheists and any other un-godly group or like-minded person that puts pressure on them to change the principles that established the United States. We have to send notice that the days of picking on the God of Abraham, Isaac and Jacob are over. The passive, love your brother, turn the other cheek is still there, BUT, now we must vote our principles and vote out anyone who does not agree. This also applies to corporations that have an agenda to change America. That's why we have freedom of choice. We can choose to purchase products and services from companies that support the principles of the Founders of our country. The Constitution is relevant today, no matter how many judges, Congress or even a President try to make it irrelevant. The principles of the Constitution are more important than any elected official. The United States is not perfect; however, it has produced the most freedom and a greater standard of living for more people than any other system in the world.

This book will give you facts so that you can stand up to people who would like to change America to what they think is better. Although they don't have any facts to prove that it would be better. Also, you would have to ask any immigrant who wants to bring their culture here: Why did you leave your country in the first place? My point is, if you like your culture so much then go back to where you came from and make your stand there. Our country was created by people that wanted the freedom we have today and were willing to give their all to make it happen. They sacrificed life, wealth, and honor to develop our country that followed the principles of the Judeo-Christian Bible to make it happen. We like these principles of our country and don't want them to be changed to something different. We have several legal ways to enter our country and to even become a citizen if you choose to. No one makes you do what you don't want to do and that is what freedom is all about. We do ask you to respect our culture and our Constitution that guides the life of our citizens. Also you are free to leave if that is not acceptable to you. No one is going to stop you from leaving.

 CALLING THE CALLED

# CHAPTER 2 - ARE YOU CALLED?

I know you may be saying "I am not sure I am called" or "Why would God want to use me?" Well, join the group! Why are you so different than say Moses (well maybe you didn't kill an Egyptian)? Moses didn't feel worthy or qualified to do what God called him to do. He even tried to convince God to use his brother Aaron whom he felt was more qualified. Moses was talking to God. Can you imagine the nerve to try to convince God not to use you? Or how about others in the Bible that appeared like they were the wrong choice?

King David – who as a boy challenged Goliath because he knew his God was greater.

Joseph – after being sold by his brothers and taken as a slave to Egypt, used his gift of interpreting dreams to become Pharaoh's right hand man.

Mary – A women chosen by God to bring our Savior into this world.

If God used a donkey to get his message out, can you believe that God can and will use YOU?

Our country is losing its Judeo-Christian heritage and principles because Christians are not standing up for what our Founding Fathers had the courage to fight and die for. They set up the greatest form of self-government that was ever created. If you don't believe that, stay with me throughout this book and challenge the facts to see if they are correct. I am an average guy who has had enough of political correctness. The effort to remove God from a country who had people that were earnestly praying to God for it to be established is insane and not justified.

People have no problem calling Saudi Arabia a Muslim nation, India a Hindu nation and China a Buddhist nation because those are the predominant religions of those nations. In my opinion, the United States was started and is predominantly a Christian nation, and those who don't like it are free to leave. As a matter of record, the United States Supreme Court in the case of the Church of the Holy Trinity vs. United States (1892), the court noted: **"No purpose of action against religion can be imputed to any legislation, State or national, because this (United States) is a religious people...This is a Christian nation."** Also John Jay, one of the Founding Fathers and the first Chief Justice of the Supreme Court said: **"Providence has given our people the choice of their rulers. It is the duty as well as the privilege and interest of our Christian nation to select and prefer Christians for their rulers."** John Adams also said **"Our Constitution was made only for a moral and religious people. It is wholly inadequate for the government of any other".** The original intent was to have people elected to serve us that were accountable not only to the people that elected them but more importantly to God. When you reference the original documents by the Founding Fathers you see that there is reference to God in judging our actions and motives. It is our duty to our country and to our future generations to elect leaders that agree with the principles of the Christian faith. When the Constitution was written, one of the most referenced books was the

Bible. It is an insult and depravity to our nation that the revisionists who rewrote the history of our country left out the influence of Christians and the principles that guided them. This is really a travesty to neglect the pain staking hours and prayers that it took for the Founders to come up with a self-governing constitution of the United States. These men and their wives sacrificed so much time, energy and money so that they could get 13 independent states to agree. For them to agree to give up some of their state powers to unite in a common central government for the greater benefit of all the states is indeed a tremendous task to say the least. Remember, at this time, there were no telephones, faxes, emails or social media's to get all the information to each citizen to ratify the Constitution. Anyone who has served on a committee and has tried to rearrange power positions, or get a complete agreement among all committee members, has an idea of the gravity of such an agreement. That is why most people who really researched the formation of the Constitution have to agree that this document had to be a divinely influenced agreement.

# CHAPTER 3 – HISTORY

The Unites States was founded on Christian principles. The more you honestly read the founding documents, written by the Founding Fathers of our great country, the more you will be convinced that this is a fact. The country's beginning can be attributed to two pastors: Wesley and Whitefield. They preached up and down the colonies to create a common spiritual bond that helped to create a national spirit. It was another pastor that further advanced this unity of the colonies churches. It was Pastor Jonathan Mayhew who met Samuel Adams and said to him "we have just had a communion of the churches, now let us have a union of the states." The idea was born.

The role of pastors influenced the decision of the Continental Congress, the Declaration of the Independence, and the Constitution. What has often bothered me was why they didn't use the name of Jesus or Christianity in the wording of the Constitution? One day while Sharon and I were talking the revelation came to me. The writers of the Constitution had separated from the British Empire which had the Church of England as its national religion. They lived in a society that had a King and a Church ruling over them. The founders wanted the Christian principles to apply to the new government without a national Church governing them individually. This is why they depended so much on prayer. Care and discussion took place to incorporate these principles into a governing document. It has to be considered a miracle because of all the different elements of the 13 colonies coming together. One major concern was that each state could have its own stated denomination of Christianity. At that time 8 of the 13 colonies had a stated religious denomination. Yet, they didn't want the federal government to endorse or recommend an individual Christian denomination. For example, when you look at the church attendance of the 55 signers of the Declaration of Independence you'll see the following: Twenty-eight were Episcopalian, eight were Pentecostal, seven were Congregationalist, two were Dutch Reform, two were Lutheran, two were Methodist, two were Catholic, and one didn't give his denomination (but he was buried and identified in a church burial), and three were Unorthodox.

When you look at the quotes used by the Founders to document many of their decisions, 34 percent of those quotes were from the Bible. Other quotes were from John Lock, an Orthodox, and Monique, a Catholic. Sir William Blackstone, Anglican, was also quoted many times in forming the Constitution. Blackstone was an English journalist in the 18th century, and he is famous for his commentaries on the "Law of England," published in 1765. This book quotes Blackstone's three types of common-law. One was Revealed Law found in the Holy Scriptures; number two was the "Law of Nature from Human Reasoning," number three was "Municipal Law, Manmade Laws." Blackstone's philosophy was that no law can contradict revealed law. These laws are to hold in check the sinful nature of people, with punishment for bad actions in breaking those laws.

The Revisionists have tried to eliminate the Christian influence in the founding of our country. Any nation that forgets its history can never be truly proud of its future. If we forget the sacrifices of the Founders, the future will always be tainted. William Gladstone said, "The teachings of Christ are the perfect solution to all the problems of society."

During the process of writing this book, one night I was awakened all through the night by the words: "Jesus is the answer; Jesus is the answer; Jesus is the answer." I kept asking, "What's the question?" Gladstone answered that best for me, and I will explain that through this book. No matter what the question, the answer is always that "Jesus is the answer."

While talking about the Constitution, let's get the facts straight about this new intellectual view of the Constitution. Today, with the Internet and 24-hour news, it is difficult for politicians to hide agendas that are many times against the will of the people. Prior to these new forms of media, bills could be passed, laws changed, and very few people knew when or how it was done. The appointment of Supreme Court Justices is a good example. How the appointees view the Constitution has a major impact on the direction of our country. During the presidential election of 2000, the difference became profound. Candidate Bush, when he talked about Supreme Court Justices, responded, "I believe that judges ought not to take the place of the legislative branch of government and that they ought to look at the Constitution as sacred. I don't believe in liberal activist judges. I believe in strict Constitutionalist judges." Candidate Al Gore countered by saying, "The Constitution ought to be interpreted as a document grows." Gore later stated, "I believe the Constitution is a living and breathing document. We have interpreted our founding charter over the years and found deeper meaning in the light of the subsequent experience in American life."

What is at stake are the principles of the Constitution. Policy and procedure can and should change, but principles are solid and should not be changed if we believe and follow the will of the Founding Fathers. What liberals and progressives refuse to accept is that the Constitution and application of it in American life has produced the greatest country in the world. That's why there is only an immigration quota. There is no exit quota.

David Barton of the Wall Builders, www.wallbuilders.com, has this to say about these two different views: "Proponents of the living constitution believe that we should not be bound by what dead white guys wrote two centuries ago, when slavery was legal, women could not vote, and horses were the fastest means of transportation. Instead, we should live under a constitution that's alive and vibrant, reflecting today's values and beliefs. Such rhetoric makes a living constitution sound appealing, but it is actually a complete mis-portrayal of the difference between the two philosophies. In reality, both accommodate an evolving society. In fact, under the strict Constitution, the original viewpoint, Article V of the Constitution requires that the Constitution be a living document. The real difference between the two approaches is not whether the Constitution should evolve, but rather how those changes should occur and who should make them. Under the living constitution approach, history and presidents are largely irrelevant. Instead, unelected judges create policy to reflect modern needs through the Constitution they themselves would write."

Having unelected judges making or rewriting laws, passed by voters, has yielded things like: it's okay to desecrate the flag, even though 80% of Americans are against this action. Or, the 90% of Americans who want to keep "Under God" in the Pledge of Allegiance. These actions are not what the Constitution and the Writers wanted the judicial branch to do. It was not designed for that. It was designed to be the least powerful branch. However, human nature continues to get more power for each branch. Each branch tries to increase the power of their branch. It's up to the legislative and administrative branch to hold them in check. Thomas Jefferson understood this. He fired one-half of the Supreme Court Justices in the early 1800s, because the Supreme Court was overstepping their boundaries and claiming more power with bad decisions. Now Congress could have reversed Jefferson's actions with two-thirds majority in each body. This is another example of checks and balances built into the Constitution. Jefferson stated, "Our Judges are as honest as other men and not more so. They have with others the same passion for party, for power, and the privilege of their corps; and their power is more dangerous as they are in office for life and not responsible as the other functionaries are to the elective control."

Finally David Barton says this about the courts' decisions: "The courts have a very poor record of protecting minority rights." Although living constitution proponents love to point to the 1954 *Brown v. Board of Education* decision that ended segregation, as proof that the courts protect minority rights. They conveniently forget to tell the rest of the story. In 1875, Congress, by the majority vote, banned all racial segregation. But in 1882, the unelected Supreme Court struck down that anti-segregation law. In 1896, the Supreme Court reaffirmed its pro-segregation position. But in 1954, the Court finally reverts itself and struck down segregation 80 years after "We the People" had abolished segregation.

What the Founding Fathers tried to accomplish with our Constitution was:

1. A federal government with limited power to do only what the individual states couldn't do for themselves and to be united.
2. Protect individual rights of each citizen by providing:
   (a) Separation of power between the three branches of government, and
   (b) Providing checks and balances to double-check and sometimes triple-check the decisions made by each branch of the new government.
3. To apply the principles of the Bible to all decisions.

The founders knew that our country had to be run by moral and ethical leaders to hold themselves in check. The basis of this was the 10 Commandments in our judicial system. That's why you see the 10 Commandments or pictures of Moses on the walls of our courts. That's why I agree with Lord Ashton who said, **"Keeping the state of government limited and in check is the responsibility of our churches."**

This is important because it is necessary to understand that every society is going to abide by someone's standards. Without standards you have anarchy. I believe every human has a *God-void* that must be filled to have a happy and productive life. I believe the Christian faith is the fulfillment for that void and for the betterment of the world. Plutarch, the promoter of Plato, said, "There never was a state of atheist. You may travel around the world and you may find cities without walls, without kings, without mint, without theater or a gymnasium, but you never find a city without God, without prayer, without oracle, without sacrifice. Some may have a city stand without foundation than a state without a belief in God. This is the bond of all society and the pillar of all our legislation."

Every colony founded has some sort of religion as their basis. We are truly blessed that the United States was founded on Christian principles that set us apart from all other civilizations. Christianity has been, and should continue to be the biggest influence in the continuing existence of our country. Not to do so would endanger the freedom of all of our children. That is why we are "calling the called" to do it now, protect what has proven to be the most free and prosperous country in the world!

Today you have to ask, "Has the US Government become so oppressive and tyrannical in the form of government that our Founding Fathers organized and fought against? Have we become the British Empire?" My answer is, not yet. However, if the leaders of our government set up unelected czars and pass rules and regulations that bypass the laws of our Constitution and our legislative process; this is exactly what will happen. We will lose our individual liberty and a British empire-type government will be established! This is to be feared by all freedom-loving Americans.

There is little question that the Founding Fathers' original intent was a centralized government with limited powers. To protect this, they established a system of checks and balances by separating the authority of the central government into three branches: The Judicial, which was established to be the least powerful, because they were not elected, but appointed; then the executive branch to be the administration to carry out the laws and directives by the legislative branch, which was designed to be the strongest because it was more directly influenced by its citizens through election.

The president is elected by an electoral college and not by the majority vote of its citizens. The taking of power by the administrative branch president is very alarming and damaging to our Constitution and our liberties. The central government was not to circumvent the power of the states. It was designed to do for the states which was not possible to do individually. For example: The monetary, the protection of all the colonies and all these states coming together. The more control the federal government takes, the less freedom states and individual citizens have. It puts the control of governing farther away from the vote of its citizens. This makes it easier for the government to become more corrupt and influenced only by a minority group of people.

What helped to move this forward was giving more authority to the judicial branch than was assigned by Congress. If Congress feels that judicial decisions are incorrect, they can reverse the Supreme Court decision by passing laws to correct their bad decisions. Revisionists have, in the name of political correctness, moved our country from the moral basis that it was founded on. The progressive attitude from the left, to be politically correct, has hurt the foundation of our country. In the name of social justice, we have created a society of takers. We have abandoned the principles of savings, sacrifice and moral conduct. This act of taking away from producers to give to non-producers will only destroy the society. The politicians that state that the Constitution of the United States only applied to the past is not what they took their oath to defend.

Finally, listen to what some of the great leaders and founders of our Constitution had to say. They are some of the people that actually wrote the Constitution. If anybody wants to know what they believed, you can go to their original letters and documents that explained their reasoning. You will see exactly what they believed. So, a lot of times, Revisionists are trying to say, "This is what I think the Founding Fathers were trying to say." To me, that is a non-intellectual approach, when you can go directly to the Founding Fathers' letters and know exactly what they were saying. Here are a few of the quotes that I think are important:

John Jay was the original Chief Justice of the United States Supreme Court. He was President of The American Bible Study and he stated: **"Providence has given to our people the choice of their rulers. It is the duty, as well as the privilege and interest of our Christian nation to select and prefer Christians for their rulers."**

Another one of the Founding Fathers was Noah Webster. He has this to say: **"Let it be impressed on our mind that God commands you to choose for rulers just men who will rule in the fear of God. If the citizens neglect their duty and place unprincipled men in office, the government will soon be corrupted. If the government fails to secure public posterity and happiness, it must be because the citizens neglected the divine command and elected bad men to make and administrate the laws."**

When we have people in office today, whose main purpose is to get reelected, instead of doing what is best for our country, our country suffers. The Founding Fathers understood human nature. They knew that our sin nature was strong and people would eventually try to do what is best for them instead of what is best for the country. That is why they wanted to put in moral people that believed in God, and knew if they did anything wrong they would have to answer to God.

Patrick Henry said, **"It cannot be emphasized too strongly or too often that this great nation was founded not by religionists but by Christians, not on religion but on the gospel of Jesus Christ."** For that reason alone, people of other faiths have been afforded freedom to worship here.

President John Adams said, **"The highest glory of the American Revolution was this: It connected in one indissoluble bond the principles of civil government with the principles of Christianity."** He also said, **"It is religion and morality alone which can establish the principles for which freedom can surely stand."**

James Madison, who penned the Constitution of the United States said, **"We have staked the whole future of our political constitutions upon the capacity of each individual to govern themselves according to the moral principles of the 10 Commandments."** Some people in our society today have opposed prayer and the posting of the 10 Commandments in our schools. Our Founders would have thought them insane to not raise our future generations without this understanding. Of the first 108 universities that were founded in America, 106 of them were founded distinctly by Christians. As a matter of fact, Harvard University, who many consider the first university in America, was founded by a

Christian named John Harvard. He was an English minister that wanted future ministers of the Gospel to have more education. He donated one half of his estate and some 350 plus volumes for the library to further this cause.

One person responsible for keeping America in line with Biblical principles was Reverend Charles Findley. He was a revivalist in the second and third Great Awakenings in America and was a college president. He had this to say: **"The time has come that Christians must vote for honest men and take consistent ground in politics. God cannot sustain this free and blessed country, which we live in and pray for, unless the church will take the right ground. Christians must do their duty to the country as part of their duty to God."** Sometimes it seems as if the foundations of this nation have become corrupt, and Christians seem to act as if they don't think God sees what they do in politics. But I tell you, He does see it. He will bless or curse this nation according to the course Christians take. There are equal consequences for action and inaction. Christians can no longer let this continue.

James Garfield lived during the early 1800's. He was the first US President that was a minister of the gospel. He stated, **"Now more than ever the people are responsible for the character of their Congress. If that body is ignorant, reckless and corrupt it is because the people tolerated ignorance, recklessness and corruption. If it be intelligent, brave and pure, it is because the people demanded these high qualities to represent them in the national legislature. If the next centennial does not find us a great nation, it will be because those who represent the enterprise, the cultural and morality of the nation did not aid in controlling the political**

**forces."** That's why we as Christians, men and women of faith who believe in God, need to be an active part of our electoral process so that we put people in office that understand that our nation was founded on these principles.

Victor Hugo said, "What you sew in schools you shall reap in the nation." Have you seen the problems that we are sewing in our schools today? Nakita Khrushchev said, "We can take over America by taking over the schools." Being a good Christian is more than reading your Bible, praying and attending church. It must include protection of our future generations. In America this is accomplished by electing representatives that truly understand what made America great. Our Founding Fathers had wisdom in knowing that to secure this freedom we must have a moral and ethical society that is grounded in Biblical principles. They knew 200 years ago that our Constitution, our freedom and our liberties had to be governed by moral people, or corrupt people would take advantage of that lost ground and use it for their own personal benefit.

Let's not screw it up! "Calling the Called" is a great commission to save America and save the benefits that we can provide for ourselves, our families, our churches, our communities and for the world. Let's make America better.

Finally let's talk about ABC – American Black Christians. You might be saying right off the bat....What's this white guy going to tell me about ABC's when he has never walked my walk. You'd be correct; however, I bet I know a bit more about the great black men and women who helped to gain a brighter future for their families than many of you. For example do you know who Prince Whipple and Oliver Cromwell were and how they served with George Washington? Did you know that Prince Whipple crossed the Delaware with General George Washington to win the first battle that turned the tide of war to the Patriots? Do you know the advantage of counting blacks as 3/5ths of a vote for representation in the Constitution was designed to actually help end slavery? How about these men?

Rev. Henry Garnet – The first African American to deliver a sermon in Congress.

Rev. Hiram Revels – The first African American to be elected to the U.S. Senate.

Joseph Rainey – The first African American to be elected to U.S. House.

Rev. Frederick Douglass – The first African American to be appointed to office in four different presidential administrations.

John Rock – The first African American admitted to the U.S. Supreme Court Bar.

The more I learned about our Christian history the more I was impressed with the Black spiritual movements. I have admired the strength of some of my Black Christian brothers until the election of Barack Obama. I was surprised to know that 95% of the black vote went to him and that in general the Democratic Party gets the majority of Black Americans vote each election. I was shocked because the Democratic Party platform supports what most Christians and the Bible are adamantly against. On the issue of abortion, Obama is in favor of the legal right to abortion, as his record indicates and his voting's supports. He has a 100% Senate voting record for years 2005-2007 from NARAL – National Abortion Rights Action League that supports all abortion rights. They are supporters of same sex marriages. On homosexual issues, this administration has repealed the ban on gays in the military and dropped the court fight to preserve the Defense of Marriage Act. As Christians we are to love the sinner, but not the sin. Homosexuality is against the teaching of the Bible; it's against nature's law and is not good for society. To promote it as a normal acceptable life style is deception. As Christians, God's laws are supreme and superior to any man made laws. The United States Constitution is the law of the land and the framers of that constitution were Christians that knew God's laws had to be part of our new country or it would never survive. If we continue to elect people who don't understand the foundation of our country and the Biblical principles that are imbedded in it, then our country will cease to be great.

Slavery was wrong and America had to work through many decades to finally keep the words of our Declaration of Independence that says **"We hold these truths to be self-evident, that all men are created equal and are endowed by their Creator with certain unalienable rights."** Slavery was one of the major challenges in uniting the states to form our union. It had to start sometime and we gradually got it right, but not without a lot of suffering and hardships. I don't want to minimize the suffering; however, I believe that this generation and the future generation of those who were sold and brought to America are so much better off than if they had been left in the country that they came from. Yes it was wrong but God can use wrong things and help them to turn out better.

I believe that most Blacks are voting out of tradition and not out of what the history has proven. Many voted for skin color instead of their Christian principles. Some of them even call other people racist but don't see the irony of what they just did. When you check the Republican Congresses and the Democratic Congresses you will see that more legislation to end slavery was blocked by the Democrats. I don't want to make this a breaking point for some of you, but if you'll look at the facts in the Congressional Records of voting on the civil rights movement, you will see a completely different story. From Abe Lincoln to Martin Luther King's marches, just look at which party blocked those bills that would give more rights to the Blacks before the 60's ended.

Finally, you know the slave mentality is not restricted to Blacks. There are plenty of whites, browns and yellows that have a slave mentality. We see it more in Blacks because of your history, but we as Christians have to break this mentality and trust more in God. A friend of mine named Mason Weaver, wrote a book titled It's OK to leave the Plantation. It's a great book for anyone who wants to change their thinking and get rid of this mindset that you are not able to change. For some, the past is extremely difficult, but the good news is that it does not have to be your future. When you reach the age of accountability you are now in charge of your future. Many successful people started life with unfair circumstances, however, they chose to forget the past, work in the present and change their future for themselves and for the benefit of their future generations. Yes, you can too. This victim mentality will always hold you back if you don't change your attitude. God is supreme and the ultimate victory is in Christ's teachings. While we are here on earth we must do all we can to make America and the rest of the world a better place to live. This can be accomplished by electing representatives that understand the history of our country and will not back away from the Christian principles that helped to form this nation. I would encourage all American Black Christians to go to www.wallbuilders.com and order the DVD – American History in Black and White. You will be blessed in the richness of your heritage. You will read about black leaders that have a totally different mentality than the Jesse Jackson's or the Al Sharpton's of this generation. You can make a major difference on how new black leaders can change the direction of the current Obama administration. We are not victims we are victors through Christ that strengthens us.

———————

## CHAPTER 4 – PASTORS - BY PASTOR RON BALL

About the author – Ron Ball is one of America's foremost public speakers. He's been speaking in front of packed crowds since the age of 15, presenting live business seminars to more than 8 million people in 21 countries. Ron has written 11 books on financial and life management with sales of two million copies. As president of Ron Ball Group, Ron Ball is a recognized business turnaround expert, teaching problem-solving strategies to more than 12,500 business people. He has spoken words of wisdom alongside such figures as Zig Zigler, former President Ronald Reagan, John Wooden, Charles Stanley, John Maxwell and many others. ron@ron-ball.com here's Ron;

My Dad has always been a lightning-rod".

Andy Stanley spoke these words after he finished his milk shake. After we had shared lunch and conversation for two hours in a popular Atlanta restaurant, I had asked Andy about his early years with his famous father, Dr. Charles Stanley, pastor of the First Baptist Church of Atlanta, Georgia and head of the world-wide *In Touch* television ministry. Andy was candid about the controversies and events of his Dad's ministry and told me dramatic stories of the moral and spiritual battles, fought by his father. When he concluded with the statement above, I asked one more question, "was it worth it"? Andy smiled and nodded yes. He then said that no upheaval or turmoil could compare with the power God had poured through that ministry as people came to Christ around the globe.

Charles Spurgeon, the giant of the English-speaking pulpit, in mid-Victorian England, was often embroiled in heated controversies connected to the urgent social and political issues of his time. One reason Spurgeon attracted the largest crowds in Britain was because he never avoided the hot topics that formed the debates of his generation.

I worked with Charles Stanley for five years as his "preaching assistant". My only responsibility was to speak when he was away. As I watched him work, I often saw parallels with Spurgeon. Both men were entirely committed to an accurate explanation of the Bible. Both men served in dynamic, world-class cities. Both men were fearless fighters for God's principles. Both men were devoted to Jesus Christ and His message of hope and salvation.

One more common element connected the two leaders. Both understood that for the church to be "salt and light" in the larger world, Christians needed to be engaged at every level of human life. They always confronted the culture with God's truth.

When I first met Charles Stanley, he invited me to his study at the original Peachtree Street church to discuss my future. The most memorable moment for me was when he relayed the story of his grandfather's influence in his early life. The grandfather, a Pentecostal minister, spent part of a year mentoring his grandson. Charles told the story with deep emotion and when he finished he said that his grandfather planted in him the pivotal, guiding principle of his life. The pastor said to the young man, "Charlie, if God tells you to go through a brick wall, you head for the wall and let God do the rest. The most important decision for the rest of your life is to always obey God and leave the consequences to Him". Charles Stanley said that he determined that obedience to God would be his commitment for the rest of his life.

I once visited a friend in Florida. He is a professional Christian counselor who divides his time between Michigan and Florida. He told me of his disappointment when he had attended a local church. He had selected the congregation because of its reputation for conservative, Biblical training. He said that in a recent Sunday morning service the pastor dealt with sexual morality. He expressed concern for the break-down of moral purity among young men and women in and out of the church. He then shocked the crowd with the assertion that the Christian faith had lost the battle for God-given sexual standards so we should accept defeat and spend our time helping teen-agers and young adults manage their sexual encounters and experiences. My friend was stunned. The pastor had given up on God's program and chosen to accommodate the popular culture. The real defeat was in his pulpit.

What you are reading is a simple request. I am asking those of you who have followed God's call into ministry to rise to the challenge of leadership. Whatever your location or situation, whether you are an American or a citizen of another country, will you stand for God and His principles of righteousness? Will you fight for the faith? Will you offer your life as a wall against the flood of reckless sin that threatens to overwhelm everyone?

The Old Testament prophet is the best example of decisive, Godly leadership. All of you are familiar with the clarity of Isaiah, the uncompromising courage of Jeremiah and the explosive power of Elijah.

Isaiah wrote, "Strengthen the feeble hands, steady the knees that give way; say to those with fearful hearts, "Be strong, do not fear; your God will come with vengeance; with divine retribution. Against whom have you raised your voice and lifted your eyes in pride? Against the Holy One of Israel!" (Isaiah 35:3-4 and 37:27).

Jeremiah recorded, "This is what the Lord says; "What fault did your fathers find in me, that they strayed so far from Me? They followed worthless idols and became worthless themselves...My people have exchanged their Glory for worthless idols. Be appalled at this, O heavens, and shudder with great horror, "declares the Lord"(Jeremiah 2:5,11-12).

God spoke directly to Jeremiah and said, "I will pronounce my judgments on my people because of their wickedness in forsaking Me. Get yourself ready! Stand up and say to them whatever I command you. Do not be terrified by them, or I will terrify you before them.... They will fight against you but will not overcome you, for I am with you and will rescue you, declares the Lord." (Jeremiah 1:16, 17-19).

Elijah confronted the wickedest political figure of his time. He openly challenged the establishment to stop their rejection of God and return to spiritual sanity. At the peak moment of his life he addressed the leaders and people of Israel. He stood tall and thundered, "How long will you waver between two opinions? If the Lord is God, follow Him..." (I Kings 18:21)

These and many other Biblical statements show that God takes disobedience and sinful actions seriously. He invariably sends a penalty for bad behavior. He judges those who reject Him.

This means that we are facing a deadly danger. When a society moves away from God, God removes His blessing and protection. In His extraordinary love and compassion He will delay disaster and give multiple opportunities to return to Him. But when that return fails to happen, judgment is inevitable. Hosea gives a sobering reminder that there are limits to God's protection, "Ephraim is joined to idols; leave him alone!" (Hosea 4:17)

What should you do now?

If you have been selected by God for spiritual leadership you have seven key responsibilities.

1.  Your first loyalty is to the Lordship of Jesus Christ over all levels of life. This does not mean that you promote a "theocracy" where Christians rule everyone else. It does mean that as Peter says in Acts 5:29, "We must obey God rather than men."

2. Explain God's principles of life and success to as many people as possible. Don't just throw words at people. Give them intelligent reasons why God's way is better. Explain why God says "no" to sex outside of a marriage relationship. Explain why God is opposed to homosexual relationships and wide-spread abortion. Explain why some things are simply wrong. Help people understand that God's regulations are for their ultimate happiness and benefit. Focus on the "why" so people will be persuaded that God's plans are superior to any alternative.

3. Aim at Biblical clarity. We are swimming in a sea of cultural confusion. The residual influence of Biblical instruction is fading in the secular arena. More and more individuals are unaware of God's standards. You can do something about that. Did you know that Focus on the Family, Canada, is not allowed to broadcast any radio shows that are critical of homosexuality or that discuss negative consequences of homosexual behavior, even if that information comes from a neutral, credible medical source? Not only is this a serious violation of free speech, it is a disservice to those who are not allowed to hear the reasons for the Christian perspective on the issue. This can happen anywhere when we abdicate our leadership and allow secularists to make the laws for society, with no balance and input from the Christian community.

4. Frame your message in love. This is not a "sappy", wimpy, sentimentalism that allows someone to think that the love of God will exempt them from consequences. This is not an attitude of false mercy that leads people to ignore God's warn-

ings. It is a strong, realistic love that genuinely cares but refuses to allow people to become irresponsible "victims".

5. Keep your personal life clear of compromise. Guard your sexual desires. Manage your money and avoid consumer debt. Celebrate your marriage. Maintain a dynamic, growing connection with God. Get help before burn-out or personal pressures push you to bad decisions with disastrous results. Stay close to your children. Be their best mentor.

6. Show clear moral leadership. Remember that politics involves free choice but requires moral direction. If we lose the battle in the political arena you may lose the freedom to lead your church. The secular system is always in competition with God. This means that you can provide the balance needed to protect the free exercise of the Christian faith. Politics is simply the means whereby organized groups of people try to get things done. If you are not involved then some of the things done may not be healthy or good for any of us. There is no contradiction between spiritual leadership and political leadership. We believe that Jesus is Lord of all of life. Make your voice heard, without it you may lose everything vital to freedom. Why would you allow secular men and women to enact laws and create policies that attack your deepest beliefs? You cannot risk our future and your freedoms by surrendering decisions to people who may not have a Biblical base for their thinking. Two important followers of Jesus, Joseph of Arimathea and Nicodemus were actually part of a political body, the

Sanhedrin, responsible for legislating local laws not determined by Judaic or Roman law. Jesus never once told them to resign their political positions.

**Ronald Reagan, in his legendary speech, *A Time for Choosing*, said, "The guns are silent in this war but frontiers fall while those who should be warriors prefer neutrality." Not too long ago two friends of mine were talking to a Cuban refugee. He was a businessman who had escaped from Castro. In the midst of his tale of horrible experiences, one of my friends turned to the other and said, "We don't know how lucky we are." The Cuban stopped and said, "How lucky you are? [At least] I had some place to escape to." And in that sentence, he told the entire story. " If freedom is lost here, there is no place to escape to." This is why you are so important. "If the trumpet does sound a clear call, who will get ready for battle?"(I Corinthians 14:8)**

7. Show some guts. In our current moral and spiritual emergency what is needed is personal courage; your courage.

   I know some of you wish you could devote yourselves to Christian ministry without the stressful demands of cultural confrontation. I wish that as well. The reality is different. You cannot know what you know about Jesus Christ, the Bible and the power of God to change people and keep it to yourself. You cannot hide while people are torn apart by a failure to follow God's directions. You are the front line that gives hope to the world, whether the world realizes it or not.

Be careful that you are not seduced by security and financial incentives to abandon your mission. Don't allow fear to replace God. As my friend Charles Stanley said in an earlier quote, "Obey God and trust the consequences to Him". Is your God big enough for that?

You are here, of course, to lead people to a personal relationship with Christ and help them mature in that relationship. But, what else are you here for? This is a time for God-called pastors and Christian leaders to stand in front of the rising tide of immorality and moral bankruptcy and say, "Stop!" This is a time for you to matter for God and His kingdom.

Winston Churchill is justifiably renowned for his vigorous courage during the dark days of the Second World War. His stirring words and unflinching determination became a catalyst for a nation on the brink of defeat. He is an example of the power and influence even one fearless, resolute leader can exert.

On June 18, 1940, Churchill gave one of his most memorable orations. It came at a time when many of the British feared the collapse of their home in the face of an imminent German invasion. Can you imagine the scene in thousands of homes as mothers and fathers gathered with their children to listen to their new Prime Minister. Churchill came to the conclusion of the speech with the words,

"Upon this battle depends the survival of Christian civilization...The whole fury and might of the enemy must very soon be turned on us...If we can stand up to him, all Europe may be free... But if we fail, then the whole world, including the United States...will sink into the abyss of a new Dark Age...Let us therefore brace ourselves to our duties, and so bear ourselves that, if the British Empire and Commonwealth last for a thousand years, men will say, this was their finest hour."

The British people stiffened. Hitler's invasion was blocked and the free world cheered the small island that had beaten the odds. One man's resolve led to critical victory.

Our challenges do not seem as desperate as those of war-threatened Britain but that is because they are camouflaged by the relative peace and security we enjoy. Without God's protection that peace and security could quickly vanish. We live in a time when the Judeo-Christian base of much of the world has been dangerously weakened. The state threatens to replace God. Power always fills a vacuum. Men and women will always seek control over other men and women. It is the message of Jesus of Nazareth and truths of the Bible that are the foundations of freedom, safety and prosperity. I encourage you to fight for God and what is right so that when your life is remembered, friends and family will say that this was your "finest hour".

# CHAPTER 5 – CHURCH LEADERS

From the time the Pilgrims left Holland to find religious freedom and evangelize the new world, pastors were the leaders in charge. Prior to the Declaration of Independence King George III of England kept putting more and more demands on the American colonies and taking more of their freedoms. He kept raising taxes and putting more pressure for the colonies to embrace the Church of England. When the time came to rally our citizens to fight for freedom, the leaders arose and became the "Black Regiment" of Pastors. It is said that the British knew the power of these pastors and targeted them for capture or death. So where are these pastors today that will risk their leadership to help change America back to its founding principles? It's a sad situation to me that so many in the leadership of our churches have been silenced for fear of losing their 501c3 status that they let the government dictate what they can say in their pulpit. If the pastors can trust God to pay their salaries, mortgages and staff, surely they can trust God to pay taxes too! Thank God there are some pastors making a stand to protect our Judeo-Christian heritage of our country. We should praise them and support them in any way we can.

The authors of our public school systems books have chosen to rewrite history and leave out the major contributions of our Christian leaders in the development of our new Republic. Anyone who would go to the

Library of Congress and read the original documents written by our Founding Fathers would not question the major impact and contributions of Christians. I thank God for people like David Barton of www.wallbuilders.com who has preserved original documents from the founding era and has made available copies to share. When you read them the facts speak for themselves.

I know many church leaders feel that their main purpose is to lead people to Christ and not to become political. I agree that salvation is the most important; however, having an environment that allows us to share, practice and apply our faith is becoming more fragile. If it is not protected it can vanish. We are the first nation that was established with the people being self-governed and the Bible was a large part of that formation. We are one if not the only country that can control our government by the people we elect to office that make the laws that govern us. If these laws don't agree with the Bible and the principles that are dear to us, we can lose the freedom to practice it. Many Christians and leaders feel that it is impossible for this to happen in the United States. They are wrong. The trend in America for the past 50 years has been to remove God from the public sector. This was never the intention of the writers of our Constitution. I know that some pastors believe and preach that God is in control and don't worry about the future. Those conditions wouldn't be here if God didn't allow it. OK but throughout scripture you read where God used other kings and kingdoms to correct the actions of His people. So it is better for us to elect leaders that understand God's principles so that God doesn't have to intervene and have a tremendous amount of pain and suffering that goes along with correction. There are corporate decisions that can cause individual blessings or punishment. We understand that when we sin it is not in Gods will for us to do that and that we have to bear the consequences. The same is true when we elect leaders that make laws contrary to Gods principals, we may out of conscience not follow the law (like abortion) however, we were part of the body that elected those people to make the laws and we will have to bear some of the corporate judgment that comes with those decisions.

Warning to church leaders: it is extremely important that you are diligent in your leadership position to watch out for deception. You must investigate what someone does, not what they say. Today's political leaders make great sounding statements to get support, and then vote opposite of what they have stated. If you are liberal in your political voting I understand your compassion for social justice and for helping the less fortunate. When candidates use these statements, it doesn't always mean that their actions are consistent with what the Bible means. President Obama is good at saying what you want to hear and doing something different. Just look at his record. I know that people will "spin" this and point to others who have done similar actions. The facts are that this administration is now in power and we have the power to vote out people that do not follow the principles established by our Founding Fathers. There is an old saying that goes like this: if you are not sure of a person's character just look at who his friends are.

"Calling the Called" is not calling for you to vote for a particular party; it is calling you to do your "due diligence" in checking the records of the people you are voting for to see if it agrees with biblical principles. If you are in a leadership position you are held accountable for your leadership decisions. You effect the lives of all those whom God has allowed you to influence. You must take this leadership position seriously and your recommendations should be screened though the Bible. It is one more cost of leadership. In some cases you may have to disagree with others in your church and even national leaders. Stand by your decisions and back them up with the research you have done. Some reference materials you can look at are: www.weeklystandard.com article by Meghan Clyne – The Green Shepherd, and also www.summit.org article by David A. Noebel, Red Advisors. There are a couple of books that are beneficial: Deceived on Purpose, by Warren Smith and Erwin Lutzer's book When a nation forgets God.

Church leaders, it is my opinion that you are doing your congregation an injustice by not educating them to do their civic and spiritual duty to investigate candidates to see what principles they follow in the decisions they make. If they believe in the principles of our Founding Fathers and the writings of our Constitution they are the type of men and women we want to serve our country. It will help them to be more honest, moral and to have a higher ethical standard. Their belief in God should put the needs of the people they represent above personal ambition and greed.

Yes, the church can be political. If your church has ever gone through a building permit process, or a zoning change it has dealt with political issues. I know that changing the direction our country is a higher calling than a church building fund, or an individual outreach program. If we lose our Christian principles that established our country in the public sector, we will surely lose it eventually in the private sector too! There will be no need for a building fund or other programs because the church will be silenced. "Calling the Called" will give you references and ideas that can help you, but your church leaders have to get involved for the sake of our communities across America. In doing so you'll not only help your community but also the communities across the world because if America falters there is no other country to go to.

We can start by encouraging our children to seek public office and be the future protectors of the principles that founded our country and the freedoms we have so far. So often you hear church leaders encouraging young people to go into ministries, missionary work, doctors and teachers to advance the world for Christ. Rarely do you hear church leaders tell youth to get involved in politics so that someday some of you will be leading your city, county, state or country in the principles that have stood the test of time. These are the people that are making the laws that we have to work under in ministry, missionary work, as doctors and as teachers. They can write laws that can limit our activities in all areas of our life. We all should be encouraging our young people to get involved in supporting candidates that have a proven record of following biblical principles. Remember not what an elected or potential office holder says, but how they actually have voted and how they run their public and private lives. What they do in private does affect how they will perform in the public arena. Don't be fooled.

P.S. Pastors or Church leaders that would like to know what they can do legally at their churches can go to www.pacificjustice.org and request a booklet free of charge. The booklet is titled: The Church and Politics: What Pastors and Churches Can Do to Affect Public Policy with Christian Principles. Or they can call 916-857-6900 and ask for this free booklet.

## Chapter 6 - FINANCES

If you were to come to our home, you would walk into our foyer and see the words in gold letters, **"As for Me and My House, We Will Serve the Lord"** [Joshua 24:15]. It is located right above the door that leads to our game room and our indoor swimming pool. Our home is set on two-and-a-half acres in the city limits and is over 6,000 square feet. We spent over $400,000.00 to update and add a 1,100 sq. ft. garage to store the rest of our vehicles. Within 48 months the house and improvements were completely paid for. Sometimes Christians may take offense at our standard of living, but let me explain that Sharon and I didn't start out this way.

Sharon and I began our lives in an apartment for the first three years of our marriage. My parents cashed in our debenture bonds, which we had earned from our business that we started before we got married, so we were able to make the down payment on our first home. It was a two-bedroom, two-bath, home totaling 1,100 square feet. We were extremely proud of this first home because it was ours, and it was the American dream to be able to own your own home. Sharon and I worked our networking business and I continued going to college. She had a full-time job working for my parents in their business. After I graduated from San Jose State University with a B.S. Degree in Accounting, our networking business had grown to a point that it surpassed the income that I could have made as an accountant. Our growing business gave us the opportunity to have our freedom as a very young couple. This freedom was not without major medical challenges.

Three weeks after our wedding, Sharon's ankles swelled to twice their original size. At first we thought it was due to the excitement and work of the wedding, setting up our own apartment and the anxiety of being on our own for the very first time. However, that was not the case. Sharon had developed a rare kidney disease called Glomerulonephritis. It was diagnosed that chronic renal failure would stop the kidney function completely. At that time, kidney transplants were uncommon and generally would only be done to head of households. Dialysis was in its developmental stages. There was no time given to how long the kidneys would last. We have been to many hospitals and tried different types of drugs to slow the failure rate.

Due to this diagnosis, the doctors recommended that we should not have children. They warned of severe risks to Sharon and the baby. Well, in our fourth year of marriage, Sharon became pregnant and the doctors recommended we abort the baby. My wife's faith-based convictions would not allow that to happen. So with great risk and prayer we were blessed to have two wonderful children. Many who watched us go through this process thought it was very challenging and yes it was. The blessing in the challenge was that I appreciated my wife so much more because I never knew how long I would have her. Plus having the faith to go through two pregnancies (our daughter Annette and our son Dennis Jr.) at such high risks was a tremendous faith builder in our spiritual lives. It was something that we had to work through early on in our marriage. We kept working through those challenges because we always believed in taking life one day at a time. We learned to praise God for our blessings while working through our challenges.

We stayed in our first home for three years. The next house we bought was a tri-level home that we stayed in for two years. We then bought a dream home at that time and stayed in it for twenty three years. During that time we invested in our business to help make our business work. Then we bought our current home. I believe in paying off your home, making wise investments, and using your abilities that God has given to you to benefit you and your family. Also to inspire others to help them become successful and move on with their lives. By taking care of your finances, I believe you can inspire people to be able to do more with their lives too.

My parents, Frank and Rita Delisle, have always inspired me to become better. Sometimes it was with tough love, and other times with generous support. I have been inspired and financially motivated by great books and great people. Dexter Yager has been a tremendous help as a friend and as a mentor in our finances and teaching us how to really love and care for people.

Robert Kiyosaki's book titled <u>Rich Dad Poor Dad</u> taught us a lot about good debt vs. bad debt. After reading it, I would advise people to be cautious about high leverage with OPM (Other People's Money), I believe that it is better to put a higher percentage of money down in your investments.

Dave Ramsey's "Financial Series" is a great system to put finances in everyday language and applications on how Christians can recover their financial lives. If you are a business owner or want to start a business, there is a difference in regard to spending money and investing money. You have to take advice from any mentor or any others and evaluate it through the current circumstances that you have in your life. In most businesses you have to work three to five years to be able to see enough profit to change your lifestyle. As Christians, we are supposed to be the "salt of the earth" by example, not by what we say but by what we do. Christians have to challenge people that believe that poverty is a way of life and to accept what God has given to you. God is an awesome God and "Everything is possible for him that believes" (Mark 9:23 NIV). You can't do the impossible by sitting at home reading your Bible and staying in a safe Bible study or a small group. I am not against any of them, of course. But, I am against expecting things to work out without doing our part in the process.

The "handout society" from the government and churches that have the "handout mindset" have to change. We have to wake up to the influence that has led us away from what we believe to be Christian principles that was adopted by our Founding Fathers; and it is being eroded by the "political correctness" in society today and the misuse of "social justice". People say, "What about the non-Christians and nonbelievers?" I say, they should support our Christian heritage, because our principles treat them with respect and allow them the freedom to worship as they wish. Many people left countries that did not allow them to worship or work as they wished to do and came to America for that freedom. Our heritage has helped to make America great. Immigrants should embrace our heritage and not try to change it. Let me get back to my point. Getting our finances in order takes guts, discipline, character, and a willingness to persevere. In my first book <u>Get it Together – Together</u>, I explained the system that we used to help us to be able to give more than ten percent, and also increase our lifestyle tremendously. Today, we invest most of our income. I have included that system below for your reading and to apply to your life to become debt free:

In the beginning, set aside a certain percentage of your income to put into two separate accounts each month. The first account is a savings/investment account and the second is a donations account. The percentage of money that you set aside is the most important starting point. People have told me that they have automatic deductions from their paychecks and that's their savings program. I do not like those programs because it lets someone else do the saving for you instead of you controlling your financial future. Once you start with the percentage, it is extremely important that you stick by that percentage until you get comfortable with it. After that, move on to the ideal percentage for your goals. The ideal goal for us is 40%, leaving 60% to spend on our lifestyle.

This is a progressive system of savings that you can grow with. Begin by writing two checks for the percentage you have established: one for your savings/investment account, and the other for God's account. Why God's account? To have true happiness, you can't build estates just for you and your family. You need a bigger picture of caring for other people. The first account is for your earthly success. The second is for your spiritual success and happiness. God doesn't need your money. You need to give the money so you don't get too hung-up on it. That's why everything needs to be in percentages instead of in dollar amounts.

When your income goes up, even though the percentage stays the same, your savings will increase. If your monthly income is $3,000 and you have decided to start with 2.5 percent for each account, you would write two checks each for $75. Write the checks and put them in your desk drawer. The money disappears from your regular checking account. The idea in writing the checks is to take the money out of accessibility for spending. Your checkbook can go $150 in the hole without causing a check to bounce because you have $150 worth of checks in your desk drawer.

Next month follow the same procedure and paper clip the two new checks to the first two checks. Continue this procedure until your checking account gets to a point where cashing the first set of checks will not cause any checks to bounce.

I had to go eight months before I could cash the first month's checks. My checkbook was always in the hole, but I never bounced a check because of the checks I held in my desk drawer.

When you cash the checks, set up two different accounts, as I mentioned earlier:

1. *God's account* should be a checking account so you can use it to give money to God's work. You could call this account a "donations" account.
2. *An investment account* should initially be in a regular savings account.

Each month, as finances permit, continue to write current checks and deposit previous checks that can be cashed without bouncing any checks. Though it may take time to do this, you will come to a point where you can write your checks for the current month and cash them at the same time. When you reach this level, raise your percentage to 5% and repeat the same procedure. At later intervals, increase the percentage to 7.5% and finally to 10%.

As your investment money increases, put part of it into higher interest CD's and then start an investment portfolio. I started with real estate and saved $3,000 to purchase a 10-acre piece of property that I could subdivide into two parcels. I arranged my payment for the balance of the land to be within the 10% I was putting into my investment account each month. The time came when I did subdivide the land, sold both parcels, and added several thousand dollars to my investment account. All profits should go right back into your investment money, which can be used to purchase more property or to make other investments.

At some point, you may need to split up your investment portfolio so you won't have all your investment money in real estate. Don't put all of your eggs in one basket! My recommendation would be three-fourths real estate and one-fourth mutual funds.

If you are self-employed, I recommend that you open a third account for taxes and insurance. Establish a percentage to be deducted from each check according to the tax bracket you are in. It is great fun to have money to invest that doesn't come from your regular checking account. It is also a wonderful feeling to have money in your donations account to use as you see other's needs or as God directs you.

An example of one of my investments was my dream of starting a U.S. National Bank. It was called Crown National Bank. After four years of satisfying the government regulators, we finally went to a stock sale in September of 1987. For the balance of our six months, we tried earnestly to sell the stock to no avail. Finally, we had to take four-and-a-half years of work and almost $500,000 and say good-bye to my chairmanship of Crown National Bank. It was a very sad time in our lives, but sixty days after closing the bank down I took my wife to Paris, France for our 20th wedding anniversary. The money I lost in the bank adventure was from our investment account. It had nothing to do with our regular checking account. Consequently, the anniversary trip was on!

It is a wonderful feeling to have money in your donations account to use as you see the need and/or as you feel God is directing you. Prior to this system, there were several times I would like to have given more, but the money was just not in our regular checking account. By having the money put into God's account, the dollars are there, regardless of what is happening in your regular checking account. It is a real blessing to see a need or feel a special calling and have the money available to give.

Isaiah 48:17 (NKJV) says: ***"I am the Lord your God, Who teaches you to profit, who leads you by the way you should go."*** Deuteronomy 8:18 (NKJV) says: ***"And you shall remember the Lord your God, for it is He who gives you power to get wealth."***

Obviously, God is interested in helping you to get it together in your finances. He wants to lead you in the financial area of your life and teach you how to profit. His investment counsel is trustworthy!

I know this procedure will work for you. It will take discipline to write the checks each month. It will take discipline not to spend the money when your investment account increases. The benefits will financially be of such a blessing it is worth all the pain of discipline.

Another benefit is the example you show your children. Delayed gratification is something that should be taught early in a person's life. You work first and then you receive. Don't get caught with a credit card every time you have a whimsical desire.'

Let's talk about when giving or charity is not really giving and charity. Let's say a person owes someone money that they borrowed or a company that issued credit to this person. Then this person gets in trouble financially and can't pay the rent. But, this person chooses to pay an offering or a tithe because he or she wants to give. They need to understand that this is just another form of stealing and can't be blessed. You are now acting like the government by taxing those people who have earned their money and giving it out to people who didn't earn it to buy votes, increase dependency, or to pay back favor for supporting their election. The tax payer may not have wanted to give to those people, just as the landlord that you didn't pay your rent to may not have chosen to support your charity. That is why it is so important for Christians to get their finances in order so that they don't have to make those type of decisions. What's important is that you give out of your own money, not what has been taken from others to distribute.

Let's expand this to party labels, let's just call them liberals and conservatives, because this mindset is in both parties. In classifying the rich, I found that most people classify rich as somebody making three times more money than them. So the term "rich" can be seen on different economic levels. So rich can be a state of mind. You cannot put your trust in the riches. Eventually, you will understand that you have to put your trust in God. But, having money for you to do what you believe God has called you to do is important in fulfilling that purpose. This will help in having a full and complete life in my estimation, because you can do more to help with financial resources than you can without them. As long as you understand and give praise to the Source, who is our heavenly Father.

Most liberals use the phrase "social justice" because they want to help all that need help, irregardless if they can help themselves. Conservatives believe in "social justice", but they believe that helping those that can't help themselves is where we should apply the money. In regards to the ones that can help themselves but choose not to, when the money is cut off and they get hungry the pain of that hunger will then create the pain of change that will create the pain of growth so that they can move on with their lives and start taking care of themselves. If somebody is continually going to give them something without any effort on their part, human nature is they are going to take it.

Shared wealth was tried by the early Pilgrims: Everybody helped everyone; they shared all their food but found that the colonies were starving. They found out that when each family was given their own plot of land to grow food that they didn't have to share and used that food to take care of their own family, they produced more. The people that couldn't work before now suddenly were able to work. That is the same human nature today that politicians don't seem to understand. Most of the successful people that I know today had to make choices in his or her life and some were very humbling. I hear people today saying, "Well that's not my expertise," or "That's below my standard," or "I won't do that". It's hard for me to understand that mentality. Sharon and I have never been afraid to clean toilets, clean ovens, clean apartments, or do whatever we had to do as a job to move ourselves forward to accomplish our dreams and goals. I believe for a person to be successful, no matter what level their income, no job or service should be beneath them. All jobs and services that move you towards your goals can and should give glory to God.

The proof to me as to whether you really believe in "social justice" is what you give out of your own money. The poor say, "If I was rich I would give more." Okay. "I say to you then, what do you give out of the money you make now? What percentage do you donate out of that income?" Example: If you make $1,000 a month, then I would encourage you to give 10% of that, or $100 a month. Well, you would say, "I don't have that money." Well, yes you do; you change your lifestyle and you do things that you have to do so that you can live on 90% and not on 100%. I would ask these people, "Do you smoke? Do you eat out? Do you drink sodas instead of water? Do you buy candy instead of buying fruits and vegetables? Do you go out to movies? Do you go on a vacation?" If you don't have the funds, it is possible to volunteer your time to charities that would equate to 10% of your income. I am not trying to judge. I am trying to explain that the power of tithing and giving to the poor start with all income levels. There is a promise that you will be blessed, because it is in the power of giving that makes life more fulfilling.

The Bible challenges us to trust God on this. Malachi 3: 10-12 (NIV) states: *Bring the whole tithe into the storehouse that there may be food in my house. Test me in this says the Lord God Almighty and see if I will not throw open the floodgate of Heaven and pour out so much blessing that you will not have room enough* for it." That is why you want to get your finances and giving in order and trust God for the results. We are to help the orphans and widowed, and those who are unable to take care of themselves to the extent they cannot.

In II Thessalonians 3:10 (NIV), Paul warns against idleness and says, *"The one who is unwilling to work shall not eat."* Also in I Timothy 5, Paul declares, *"Anyone who does not provide for their relatives, and especially for their own household has denied the faith and is worse than an unbeliever."* Having our finances in order helps us to give with a happy heart. We give to charities because it's right and makes us feel great. God knows our heart, and charity is a heart-issue. So having your finances in order frees you up to enjoy this blessing. That is why it is hard to feel charitable when the government taxes money away from its citizens, then tries to be charitable with that money that they have taken from you. It no longer is a heart issue; it feels more like a thief has stolen your money.

Politically, who are the givers? The liberals, mostly Democrats, would like you to believe that they are the party of givers. They sound more compassionate and generous in helping the poor. But talk is cheap. You have to look at the facts. First, it is always easier to spend somebody else's money rather than your own. When politicians dish out money, it is money that they have taken from us in taxes. When people say, "It's the government's money," it really isn't. The money that politicians are giving away is your money and mine. The truly conservative, mostly Republicans, would let you keep more of your money and have you give to whom you choose to give to. I know this statement will turn off party loyalists, but you have to be open-minded and look at the facts. Arthur Brooks, the author of the book <u>Who Really Cares</u> documents the following facts (you can check these out for yourself):

*"It turns out that conservatives give about 30% more than liberals."* He adds, *"And, incidentally, conservative-headed families make slightly less money per year than liberal-headed families."* Brooks also noted church membership was a major factor. A person's charitable giving is directly related to their religious participation. The religious give up to four times or 400% more than non-religious to charity. This giving is also reflected in other donations like community efforts, blood drives, etc. It is reported that if liberals donated blood at the same rate of conservatives, the blood banks would increase by 45%. All-in-all, charitable giving helps you to defeat greed. When you have learned to give from your heart, you realize that the blessings are there to be shared.

## Chapter 7 – THE FIRST AMENDMENT TO THE CONSTITUTION

This is the age of revisionists rewriting our history to try to explain what the writers of the Constitution were saying. All these intellectuals need to do is go to the Founders' actual writings in the Congressional Records to see their actual intent. A revisionist, who doesn't use original writings, are at best ignorant, or at worst trying to put into place an agenda that fits their beliefs as opposed to the truth of what the Founders wanted.

The writers of the Constitution were extremely dedicated to getting an agreement that would produce a successful union. However, they knew that they may not have gotten everything perfect, so they allowed a way to change the document by the amendment process.

The first 10 amendments to the Constitution are called the Bill of Rights. These were passed to protect the liberties of the individuals by adding these amendments so that the New Government would only do what the states allowed them to do. The states wanted to protect their sovereignty. Over the years, Revisionists have tried and are succeeding at changing the original intent of the authors. The worst of these intents are in regard to the First Amendment, which reads:

**"Congress shall make no law respecting an establishment of religion or prohibiting the free exercise thereof, or abridging the freedom of speech or of the press; or the right of 'The People' peaceably to assemble, and to petition the government for their grievances."**

The best way to clarify any conflict in the meaning of the First Amendment would be to go to the Congressional records from June 7th to September 25th, 1789. This contains the complete discussion of the Founding Fathers surrounding their formation of this Amendment.

The confusion and misinterpretation of this was started by the Supreme Court's decision in the court case titled _Everson v. Board of Education_ in 1947. The Court in the past has always used precedents and preceding court cases to help in the clarification of the statutes in making their decisions. In the _Everson_ case, the phrase: "Separation of Church and state" was used to influence the Justices. But where did this phrase come from? Most people believe it is in the Constitution. It is not. The phrase actually comes out of a private letter from Thomas Jefferson writing to the Danbury Baptist Association of Connecticut, who was trying to explain to them that the New Government would not establish a national denomination of the Christian faith. Why the concern? It was because at that time the states could endorse a religion. For example, eight out of the 13 Colonies had state religions. The 8 state endorsements were: Virginia, New York, Maryland, North Carolina and South Carolina were with the Anglican Church, which was the Church of England. Massachusetts, Connecticut, and New Hampshire were Congregationalists in their beliefs.

Because the majority of the states had the Anglican denomination as their state denomination, this concerned the Baptists. The other denominations were very concerned that like the British Empire, the Church of England would become the national church, with a king as the leader just like Britain. They surely did not want that in America because they already fought that battle for their freedom to have the right to worship in their chosen denomination. So, that is why Jefferson wrote the letter to the Danbury Baptist Association, telling them that the First Amendment has built a wall of separation between Church and state, and that it would prevent a nationalization of one specific denomination.

The ACLU and the Revisionist judges used Jefferson's personal and private letter to change the meaning of the First Amendment. Yet you don't hear the ACLU using other quotes for Jefferson like the ones that follow:

**"The democracy will cease to exist when you take away from those who are willing to work and give to those who would not."**

**"It's incumbent on every generation to pay its own debts as it goes. A principle which is acted on would save one-half the wars of the world.**

**"I predict future happiness for Americans if they can prevent the government from wasting the labors of the people under the pretense of taking care of them."**

**"The strongest reason for the people to retain the right to keep and bear arms is, as a last resort, to protect themselves against tyranny in government."**

"To compel a man to subsidize with his taxes the prop-
agation of ideas which he disbelieves and abhors is
sinful and tyrannical."
"My reading of history convinces me that most bad
governments result from too much government."

Thomas Jefferson was a tremendous Founding
Father but was not the best source to be used for understanding the First Amendment. He was not one of the
55 participants at the Constitutional Congress, neither
was he one of the 90 congressmen that actually wrote
the First Amendment. It would have been more accurate to quote some of the Founders that were actually
there. For example, quoting Gouverneur Morris, who
was a participant at the Continental Congress would
have been more applicable. He states,

**"Religion is the only solid basis of good morals,
therefore education should teach the precepts of
religion, and the duties of man towards God."**

Then consider Fisher Ames of Massachusetts, who
provided the wording for the First Amendment that
was passed by the House of Representatives. He would
certainly know the intent of that amendment, yet you
never hear him use the phrase, "Separation of Church
and state." He called the Bible the primary textbook in
our American classrooms that should always remain.

**"Should not the Bible regain the place it once
held in our school books? Its morals are pure, its
examples captivating and noble. The reverence
for the sacred book that is thus early expressed**

lasts long; and probably, if not impressed in infancy, never takes firm hold in the mind."

Or you may want to use the great example of George Washington. Most people understand that without George Washington we would not have a country today. In George Washington's Farewell Address, he states:

"Of all the dispositions and habits, which lead to political prosperity, religion and morality are indispensable supports. In vein would that man claim the tribute of patriotism who should labor to subvert these great pillars? The mere politician equally with the pious man, ought to respect and cherish them...let it simply be asked, where is the security for property, for reputation and for life if the sense of religious obligation is deserted... and let us with caution indulge the supposition that morality can be maintained without religion. Whatever may be conceded to the influence of refined education on minds...reason and experience both forbid us to expect that nation morality can prevail in exclusion of religious principles."

Another Founding Father, Patrick Henry stated:

"The Bible is a book worth more than any other books that were ever printed."

Noah Webster stated:

"The Bible is the chief moral course of all that is good and best correctors of all that is evil in

**human society; the best book for regulating the temporal (secular) concerns of men."**

John Jay was the original signer of both documents. He was the original Chief Justice of the United States Supreme Court. He stated:

**"The Bible is the best of all books, for it is the Word of God and teaches us the way to be happy in this world and in the next. Continue, therefore, to read it and to regulate your life by its precepts."**

There is no other record of any of the other Founding Fathers ever using the phrase, "Separation of Church and state." If they wanted them truly separated, these men would have known so. There is absolutely no doubt that when you read the writings from the Founding Fathers that they wanted to protect religious freedom and wanted to keep God in our schools, our public areas, our government, and in our personal lives.

## Chapter 8 - EDUCATION

Boy, have we strayed far away from what education was intended to do for our society. Remember, each society followed some spiritual belief in its history. In the discovery and the formation of the Americas and the United States we see that Christopher Columbus was a Christian whose mission was the spreading of the Gospel. This was recorded in Christopher Columbus' own journal.

**"It was the Lord who put into my mind – I could feel His hand upon me – the fact that I could sail from here to the Indies. All who heard of my project rejected it with laughter, ridiculing me. There is no question that the inspiration was from the Holy Spirit, because He confronted me – waves of marvelous inspiration from the Holy Scriptures."** **(1492)**

The Pilgrims, who sought religious freedom and to spread the Gospel to the early settlers in America, also had strong religious convictions. Each settlement concerned about their future generations taught their children at home and set up educational opportunities that were mostly headed by the pastors of their local churches. Pastors tended to be the most educated and most influential people in society. They had the double-duty of educating and pastoring their congregation in spiritual issues as well as issues that affected their community.

Notice they were called educators. Today they are called teachers. I think it is because educators taught children "how to" think with moral and ethical values as part of their education. Whereas, teachers today teach what administrators want them to think and it does not always agree with parents and Christian principles. But that is only my opinion. We should educate more on how to solve problems, how to analyze information and how to check other sources. It should also include the moral aspect of the consequences of bad actions. Then people will be able to form their own opinions based on the information that they have gathered. Most of our higher education today comes with a liberal bias. This is in conflict with the Founders of our country that taught personal responsibility, strong work ethics and rewards. These were based on what was done not what the government gave you or what people felt they were entitled to. We have to change this mentality to move our country back to its foundations.

Most of the American colonies were established by Christians from different denominations. Many of the schools started in providing higher Christian education that could not be taught in their homes or churches. They knew that liberty and justice had to have the moral basis that the Christian faith provided. Benjamin Franklin said:

**"A nation of well-informed men, who have been taught to know and prize the rights which God has given them, cannot be enslaved. It is in the region of ignorance that tyranny begins."**

When Revisionists rewrote our history, they left out any reference to Christianity. This is a tremendous error, and a slap in the face to all of those Christians who died for the liberties that the Revisionists have today. One major founding father that is not well-known, because of his strong Christian conviction and influence, is Benjamin Rush. He was the signor of the Declaration of Independence and the Constitution. He was also a Professor of Medicine. He was also called the Father of Public Schools, and he said this:

**"In contemplating the political intuitions of the United States, I lament that we waste so much time and money in punishing crimes and take so little pains to prevent them. We profess to be Republicans, and yet we neglect the only means of establishing or perpetuating our Republican form of government. That is the universal education of our youth and the principle of Christianity by the means of the Bible. For this divine book, above all others, favors equality among mankind, respect for just laws, and those sober and frugal virtues, which constitute the soul of Republicanism."**

**"The number one purpose of public schools is to teach youth, young people, the Word of God."**

**"If we are ever to arrive at a point in America where our schools only deal with intellect and ignore the spirit, if we just train the mind and don't train the character, all we would have done is release on America a group of educated criminals."**

You can clearly see his intent for public education differs from today's misguided notion that you have to take God out of our schools.

As a matter of fact, of the first 108 colleges, 106 were formed on the Christian faith and by Christian denominations. Harvard, becoming the first in these higher educations in 1638, was founded by John Harvard, a Congregationalist with a donation of one-half of his estate and 320 books from his library. For the early students of Harvard, it was noted that each student was told this:

**"Let every student be plainly instructed and earnestly pressed to consider well the main end of this life and studies is: 'To know God and Jesus Christ, which is eternal life', John 17: 3, and, therefore, to lay Christ in the bottom, as the only foundation of all sound knowledge and learning.'"**

Other earlier colleges that were formed from their church affiliations are: 1693, the College of William and Mary. It was started by the Episcopalians; 1700, Yale, started by the Congregationalists; 1746, Princeton, started by the Presbyterians; 1759, Columbia, started by the Episcopalians; 1764, The Brown University, started by the Baptists, and 1770, Rectors, started by the Dutch Reform Church. Many of these Christian denominations wanted to teach the principles of their denomination by the colleges that they supported. But all had the goal of protecting their freedom and liberty with the foundation of Christian principles as their main purpose.

The Founders of this great nation knew this and said so. James Madison was known as the Father of the Bill of Rights. So he really understood the First Ten Amendments. Especially the First Amendment that is so misunderstood today. Then he quotes here:

**"We have staked the whole future of American civilization not on the power of government, far from it; we have staked the future of all of our political institutions upon the capacity of each and all of us to govern ourselves to the Ten Commandments of God."**

James Wilson was a signor of the Declaration of Independence and the Constitution. There are only six people that have signed both of these beginning documents. He also was one of the justices of the Supreme Court, and said:

**"Human law must rest in its authority, ultimately in the laws that are divine."**

All of these institutions valued education based upon the moral and ethics of their Christian faith. Many of the Founding Fathers, who were educated in these institutions, understood that knowledge without a spiritual base meant their education was not complete. Such are the statements of some of the other Founding Fathers. John Adams said:

**"It is religion and morality alone which can establish the principles on which freedom can securely stand."**

Finally, the Founding Fathers believe that Church and government are both instruments whereby God would combat sin, the Church had its role and function, and the governments had its role and its function. Both were meant to curtail and keep sin in check. Laws were made to prevent bad moral and ethical actions. Punishment would result for wrong actions to protect society. Most people today believe the root of our country's problem is in the lack of morals and virtue, the principles that are rooted in the Christian faith. Yet we have atheists and the ACLU members that are filing lawsuits to take these proven principles out of our schools and out of our public square to the detriment of our country. Schools cannot display the Ten Commandments because the Supreme Court has ruled that it might influence our children. Things like: "Thou shall not steal." "Thou shall not bear false witness." "Thou shall honor thy father and mother." "Thou shall not kill." I think it is pretty stupid for the Supreme Court to say that they would not want our kids to be influenced by this! What parent or person of reason would not want these Commandments influencing the lives of their children?

At this time of writing there was an email by an unknown author called the GRAY-HAIRED BRIGADE that I felt was worth ending this chapter with.

"THEY LIKE TO REFER TO US AS SENIOR CITIZENS, OLD FOGIES, GEEZERS, AND IN SOME CASES DINOSAURS. SOME OF US ARE 'BABY BOOMERS' GETTING READY TO RETIRE. OTHERS HAVE BEEN RETIRED FOR SOME TIME. WE WALK A LITTLE SLOWER THESE DAYS AND OUR EYES AND HEARING IS NOT WHAT THEY ONCE WERE.

WE HAVE WORKED HARD, RAISED OUR CHILDREN, AND WORSHIPPED OUR GOD AND GROWN OLD TOGETHER. YES, WE ARE THE ONES SOME REFER TO AS BEING OVER THE HILL, AND THAT IS PROBOBLY TRUE. BUT

BEFORE WRITING US OFF COMPLETELY, THERE ARE A FEW THINGS THAT NEED TO BE TAKEN INTO CONSIDERATION.

IN SCHOOL WE STUDIED ENGLISH, HISTORY, MATH, AND SCIENCE WHICH ENABLED US TO LEAD AMERICA INTO THE TECHNOLOGICAL AGE. MOST OF US REMEMBER WHAT OUTHOUSES WERE, MANY OF US WITH FIRSTHAND EXPERIENCE. WE REMEMBER THE DAYS OF TELEPHONE PARTY-LINES, 25 CENT GASOLINE AND MILK AND ICE BEING DELIVERED TO OUR HOMES. FOR THOSE OF YOU WHO DON'T KNOW WHAT AN ICEBOX IS, TODAY THEY ARE ELECTRIC AND ARE REFERRED TO AS REFRIGERATORS. A FEW EVEN REMEMBER WHEN CARS WERE STARTED WITH A CRANK. YES, WE LIVED THOSE DAYS.

WE ARE CONSIDERED OLD FASHIONED AND OUTDATED BY MANY. BUT THERE ARE A FEW THINGS YOU NEED TO REMEMBER BEFORE COMPLETELY WRITING US OFF. WE WON WORLD WAR II, FOUGHT IN KOREA AND VIETNAM. WE CAN QUOTE THE PLEDGE OF ALLEGIANCE, AND KNOW WHERE TO PLACE OUR HAND WHILE DOING SO. WE WORE THE UNIFORM OF OUR COUNTRY WITH PRIDE AND LOST MANY FRIENDS ON THE BATTLEFIELD. WE DIDN'T FIGHT FOR THE SOCIALIST STATES OF AMERICA; WE FOUGHT FOR THE 'LAND OF THE FREE AND THE HOME OF THE BRAVE.' WE WORE DIFFERENT UNIFORMS BUT CARRIED THE SAME FLAG. WE KNOW THE WORDS TO THE STAR SPANGLED BANNER, AMERICA, AND AMERICA THE BEAUTIFUL BY HEART AND YOU MAY EVEN SEE SOME TEARS RUNNING DOWN OUR CHEEKS AS WE SING. WE HAVE LIVED WHAT MANY OF YOU HAVE ONLY READ ABOUT IN HISTORY BOOKS AND WE FEEL NO OBLIGATION TO APOLOGIZE TO ANYONE FOR AMERICA. YES, WE ARE OLD AND SLOW THESE DAYS BUT REST ASSURED, WE HAVE AT LEAST ONE GOOD FIGHT LEFT IN US. WE HAVE LOVED THIS COUNTRY, FOUGHT FOR IT, AND

DIED FOR IT, AND NOW WE ARE GOING TO SAVE IT. IT IS OUR COUNTRY AND NOBODY IS GOING TO TAKE IT AWAY FROM US. WE TOOK OATHS TO DEFEND AMERICA AGAINST ALL ENEMIES, FOREIGN AND DOMESTIC, AND THAT IS AN OATH WE PLAN TO KEEP. THERE ARE THOSE WHO WANT TO DESTROY THIS LAND WE LOVE BUT, LIKE OUR FOUNDERS, THERE IS NO WAY WE ARE GOING TO REMAIN SILENT.

IT WAS THE YOUNG PEOPLE OF THIS NATION WHO ELECTED OBAMA AND THE DEMOCRATIC CONGRESS. YOU FELL FOR THE 'HOPE AND CHANGE' WHICH IN REALITY WAS NOTHING BUT 'HYPE AND LIES.' YOU HAVE TASTED SOCIALISM AND SEEN EVIL FACE TO FACE, AND HAVE FOUND YOU DON'T LIKE IT AFTER ALL. YOU MAKE A LOT OF NOISE, BUT MOST ARE ALL TOO INTERESTED IN THEIR CAREERS OR 'CLIMBING THE SOCIAL LADDER' TO BE INVOLVED IN SUCH MUNDANE THINGS AS PATRI-OTISM AND VOTING. MANY OF THOSE WHO FELL FOR THE 'GREAT LIE' IN 2008 ARE NOW HAVING BUYER'S REMORSE. WITH ALL THAT EDUCATION WE GAVE YOU, YOU DIDN'T HAVE THE SENSE ENOUGH TO SEE THROUGH THE LIES. NOW YOU ARE PAYING THE PRICE AND COM-PLAINING ABOUT IT. NO JOBS, LOST MORTGAGES, HIGHER TAXES AND LESS FREEDOM. THIS IS WHAT YOU VOTED FOR AND THIS IS WHAT YOU GOT.

WELL, DON'T WORRY YOUNGSTERS, THE GREY-HAIRED BRIGADE IS HERE, AND IN 2012 WE ARE GOING TO TAKE BACK OUR NATION. WE MAY DRIVE A LITTLE SLOWER THAN YOU WOULD LIKE BUT WE GET WHERE WE'RE GOING, AND IN 2012 WE'RE GOING TO THE POLLS BY THE MILLIONS. THIS LAND DOES NOT BELONG TO THE MAN IN THE WHITE HOUSE OR TO THE LIKES OF PELOSI AND REID. IT BELONGS TO 'WE THE PEOPLE' AND WE PLAN TO RECLAIM OUR LAND AND OUR FREEDOM.

WE HOPE THIS TIME YOU WILL DO A BETTER JOB OF PRE-
SERVING IT AND PASSING IT ALONG TO OUR GRAND-
CHILDREN. SO THE NEXT TIME YOU STAND AND HONOR
OUR COUNTRY REMEMBER TO THANK GOD FOR THE
'GREY-HAIRED BRIGADE."

---

## CHAPTER 9 - FREE ENTERPRISE-CAPITALISM

*For this chapter, I was given permission by the Honorable Bob McEwen to insert a speech he gave at a "Free Enterprise Weekend."*

This is called a Free Enterprise Weekend. And free enterprise traditionally has been explained in all of our weekends by Rich DeVos for many, many years. It is now proven to be my privilege to remind us as to why some places are rich, why some places are poor, how it works, what free enterprise means, and the very, very essential part that you play in it. There is an underlying principle of free enterprise that is different from socialism. Socialism is government control. Free enterprise is individual control.

It was March 23, 1774 when the people that were in the Colony of Virginia, who were still under the British crown as America had not been formed yet, decided to call upon God for Wisdom; because the Bible says that when you don't know something you can ask God for guidance. And so Richard Henry Lee, Patrick Henry and Thomas Jefferson wrote a Resolution in which they would call the entire Colony of Virginia to spend a day of fasting and prayer – May 23, 1774. The very next morning the King's representative, Governor Dunmore, came storming into the House of Burgess's where they were meeting, and he was waving that Resolution over his head. He was very, very offended that these people thought they could talk directly to God and not go through the King. And even more so, not go through the King's representative, the governor. He got so mad and so offended that they hadn't gone to him first, but had gone directly to God that he closed the House of Burgess. He said, "You people are not entitled to even meet. I am going to stop this representative body of the people of Virginia. You are finished. You are going to do what I say!"

In the back of the room was a representative from Fairfax County Virginia. His name was George Washington. And he said, "Men, follow me." And they went down the street to a tavern. I call it a Holiday Inn, because it had sleeping rooms above and a restaurant below. They met there and they reviewed the Resolution that Thomas Jefferson and Patrick Henry had written. But then they did this: They said, "We understand that we need to have a gathering of all of the Colonies." And so they called for the First Continental Congress, a meeting of the Representatives, where they wrote for the very first time using the phrase "a meeting of the United States of America to bring all of the states together, based upon an idea that there is a God, that He made us, and that we are accountable to Him."

When you see yourself as an individual special creation, then it is very hard to make a person like that submissive. They become independent, they become creative, and they become prosperous. That is what free enterprise is about. It's about people that can do things for themselves, that believe in individual responsibility and with it comes individual accountability. That is what we are going to talk about over these next couple of minutes. What is free enterprise? What is profit? And does profit matter? How is wealth created? Is it created or is it distributed? What is a business? And, finally, what part do you play in this, and can you do it? And then there are some closing thoughts.

Free enterprise requires two things. It requires freedom of choice and private property. You have to own it. And then you also have to have a profit, which is a reward. What is free enterprise? Free enterprise is doing something good for others, making their life better and receiving reward for doing it. It's an economic system whereby people are rewarded for doing good things for other people. As a consequence, under free enterprise, is where the goodness – the things that we enjoy come from. People were uncomfortably hot for a long time. We are very thankful that Willis Carrier invented the air-conditioner. And why did he do that? He made life better for other people so that you and I could reward him. That is why we would reach into our pocket and say, "We would rather be nice and cool and comfortable than have these dollars." And so we buy an air-conditioner.

Charles Goodyear decided that he had this rubber plant, and it had this sap in it. When it got cold it would get brittle and break. And when it got hot it would be stringy and syrupy. He had this idea that he could make something useful out of that sap. So he spent all of his life trying to figure out a way to do it. He wasn't making much income, and the Court was going to take his children away from him, because he wasn't providing for them. So his brother-in-law came to the little shack where he lives. He had a pot-bellied stove there, and his brother-in-law came and was lecturing him, and he said, "You should go out and get a job." He said, "You are trying to invent this thing and create this thing." He said, "It's not going to work. Trying to make a useful thing out of this sap is like trying to make a chair fly. You can't do it!" And Charles Goodyear said, "I am convinced that either by accident or design someone will find a use for rubber."

Now what he had done, among other things, was that he had mixed sulfur with the rubber juice and he was standing there – and as he was arguing with his brother-in-law, he was heating it over the pot-bellied stove. And some of it boiled off and it landed on the stove. As he went back and scrapped the rubber off he discovered that where it had burned on the stove that it kept its consistency; it didn't change. We call that system vulcanization. That is, you take rubber, you add sulfur to it and you heat it and it maintains its shape.

Inventions, creations and benefits come from people who are allowed to have a reward. And as a consequence, we all are better off. And what about the record player? Thomas Edison invented the record player. Everybody in the world had a record collection until some Americans invented the compact disc. And that was the end of the record business. And then everybody had a compact disc until somebody invented the iPod. And the iPod made it possible for the first time – something that you and I have always wanted to do – to buy the songs that we actually want and not the 12 and 15 that are on a single CD, or the 15 or 20 that are on a single record. We can actually buy the one that we want.

And with each new step of a new invention, under free enterprise, where I figure out what other people want, where I bless them and I then receive a reward;

and that is what free enterprise is. It creates the blessings that we enjoy. Socialism doesn't do that. Socialism is when government tells you what to do. Let's take an example of socialism. It could be a prison. In a prison, you don't have choice. That is, they decide what you are going to eat; they decide when you are going to get up. And if you invented anything or made anything any better you wouldn't get rewarded for it. So what do they do? Nobody invents anything. Nobody creates anything. In fact, the only thing they do is sit and fight. So there is a benefit. Freedom creates abundance.

So what is the blessing that we receive in return? When people reach in their pocket to say thank you for what they have done for them that provides a benefit that is called "a profit." Now you will hear some of these folks, especially the ones recently on television up there at Wall Street, they are talking about evil profit. Well, let me explain. Without profit there is no invention, there is no creation, there are no products, and there is no blessing. Profit is the message that is sent to producers to make something. Let me give an example. Let us suppose that all of the water and all of the concession sales had been shut off in this building so that you hadn't had any water or any access to any water since 8 o'clock this morning. Now, there would be a strong desire to have some water. So if someone ran across the street and they got a few cases of water at $1.00 a bottle, there are a lot of us in this room that by this time in the afternoon, having gone all this time, we would pay $5.00 for a bottle of water. And if you sold 100 of those, you'd make $500 right then! Somebody sitting around here would say, "Oh, my goodness. He made $4.00 on each one of those. I am going to run and grab some, and they are selling them for $5.00

over here at this door," he said, "I'll sell them over here for $4.00." And he would make $300 real quick. And everybody would run and get the water and solve the problem. And the price would continue to come down until there was equilibrium, and then it would be like it is right now. Nobody needs anymore water. Everybody is content.

What does profit do? Profit calls forth the good that is needed and the higher the profit the more the encouragement to create it. And then as more is created the profit diminishes, and it says we don't need anymore, until finally there is no profit at all. When there is no profit at all they don't make any more. Are you with me? This is because this is a fundamental, central ingredient of free enterprise. There has to be a profit. And without a profit there is no business. There is no reward. There are no benefits.

Let me hit it one more time. If you get on Interstate 70 and you drive east of here for a couple of hours you come to a place called Columbus, Ohio. Now let's suppose that there is a shortage of apartments and places to live in Columbus. How would you know that? That is because people would pay a great deal for one of the apartments that is available, and people might be able to make $500 or $600 a month on an apartment. Now that word would get out to the folks in Cleveland, Toledo, Indianapolis, Louisville, and they would say, "Do you realize I am making $100 a month on my apartments? They are making $500 a month up in Columbus." So what would they do? They would go and build some apartments. When they built the apartments the profit-motive has encouraged. As more of them come in you then see the price goes down, because now you have more opportunities until it begins to balance itself. That is what profit does. It calls for a need for something, and when there is adequate supply there is no more profit. It is the message that is sent out to the marketplace. And anybody who wants to get rid of profit means that they are getting rid of the production. And so if some politician says that oil companies should not make a profit, then an oil company would say, "Why should I drill for oil?" And then there would be a shortage of oil.

That, ladies and gentlemen, in a picture is called socialism. It does it to everybody. For example, in Cuba, which was the second or third richest nation in the western hemisphere until Castro came in and began to say, "You can't make a profit. I will see how much it costs to make a cigar. I'm going to take all the rest of the money in taxes. I see how much it costs to have a chicken farm; I'm going to take the rest in taxes." So there was no profit, therefore there was no production, and the economy collapsed as, indeed, it always will.

Chile in the 1970's was taken over for a brief period by the Communists. They said, "Everybody should be paid the same. The guy that comes in early and works harder, he shouldn't get any more than this person. Everybody gets the same paycheck." Everybody said, "Well, in that case, watch this." And so the production in the copper mines fell 70% in the first 30 days, in just less than a month, without profit to encourage people to produce there was no production. And, of course, everyone is worse off.

Under free enterprise people are awarded in the degree to which they bless someone else. That is where wealth, hope and opportunity are created. When that is denied people, they don't get it. I was getting on the plane the other day and my son said to me, "There is an app for your phone that will tell you all you have to do. It will lock onto your reservation and when you land it will show you a little picture of the airport. It will show you where your gate is, and the plane that you are transferring to, where that gate is so that you will know immediately where you are. If you are in a hurry you won't have to run around and find out what the monitor says. In fact, it will show you where the little bus goes this way, or the tram goes that way, and which one is the quickest. You can sit there on the plane and figure that all out. The application costs 99 cents." Now the question is: is that worth 99 cents to have that on my phone for the next several years? Absolutely! But why did this person whom I don't even know – it could be a left-handed female from Argentina, do this? I have no idea who it is. But, it doesn't matter under free enterprise. Under free enterprise we don't care. We care about the quality of the product. We don't focus on people. People are all equal in the eyes of God, and in free enterprise everyone has equal opportunity. No specialties for anybody who comes from a certain blood line or a certain characteristic. In free enterprise, anybody can produce and anybody is rewarded. And whoever did that, why did he do that? He created that application hoping that a million people like me would download that and a million people times 99 he would be a millionaire for having made that piece.

That is why the freedom, that is why the abundance, that is why the free countries are the places where people live so well. Now what does that have to do with you? And that is why you are essential. A person is rewarded in direct proportion to his contribution to others. Under free enterprise, the more people you bless, the greater your reward. One way that you bless other people is called personal service. Personal service is something that you do for someone else. You do it physically, and you do it by performing a task and you are usually paid by the hour.

Now here is what is interesting about this: You are rewarded based upon the quality of the task. People reward you for the task that you are doing. So let us suppose that you want the snow shoveled from your front sidewalk. So the task is worth to you maybe $4 or $5. And the person comes from next door, and he knocks on your door and he says, "I would like to shovel your snow." You say, "Well that's good." I'll pay $5 for that. And he says, "No, no, no. Don't you understand who I am? I'm a doctor, and I have five children, and I have a mortgage, and I can't live on $5," and he gets very irate. See the important thing is, it is not the value of the person; the person is invaluable in the sight of God. We are rewarded based upon the task. If a person can only perform certain tasks, then he is disappointed in the value that he can create. There is a way to increase his performance, a way to increase his contribution. That is called a business. A business is something that takes this capacity and multiplies it by gathering people together.

Now there are three people that do that. And these three people are very, very important. One is called a saver. That is a person that gathers the money necessary to accomplish something. The second one is you, called the entrepreneur. The entrepreneur is the person that takes the money that creates the business. The third person allows producers or workers to make something. Now, let me simply say, all wealth is created by these three people. All wealth comes from these three people. A nation that honors these people becomes wealthy. A nation that attacks these people becomes poor. And that is where it is essential for all of us to understand, because the degree to which you attack these people – you can take a rich country and make it poor.

There is an organization called the Index of Economic Freedom. The Index of Economic Freedom shows how much abuse is given to each one of these three. Here is the principle: the greater the freedom the greater the wealth. How would you hurt these people? By imposing taxes, that is you take money away from them. And when you take money away from them, then they don't produce, and the nation becomes poorer. Currently, number two, out of the second richest in the world, according to this, and it comes out every year, is Singapore. Number three is Australia. Number four is New Zealand. Number six is Canada. Now Canada used to be number twelve. And over the last few years, Canada has gone from twelve to six. America used to be number one. Now America is number nine. In the process of us making decisions, you can make any poor place rich. You can make the right decisions by awarding these people who put together a business in order to bless other folks; the degree to which they do that is a degree to which nations prosper.

Now why is that important to you? Remember my principle: The greater the contribution the greater the reward? There are many, many people all over the globe that are tied at performing a task in which they are infinitely more qualified, but they are stuck putting on that one little wrench or doing this one little thing, or maybe not even having a job at all. And someone who cares about them, someone who is an entrepreneur, someone who decides that they are going to put their arm around this person and show them how they can go into business for themselves, so that they are not at the mercy of the individual task, but they are able to build an organization that is able to bless more and more people, and the more people they bless, the wealthier they become. In our business here, that is what an Emerald is, that's what a diamond is, and that is what a Founder's Diamond is. The more people they bless, the more people they help, the more people they recruit, the wealthier they perform. Now that is the key to freedom, that's the key to wealth: People who do what you are doing.

Eighty percent of all of the wealth in America that is created is done by small businesses, individuals. Now let me just explain why that would be. In a big business, if you want to gather an idea, and that idea is not working and you then have to go to your boss, and your boss has to get approval from this person, and by the time they make all the changes you have missed the mark. At a small business, working out of their garage or out of their front store, they can make those changes rapidly. This only works every time. This is always the way that it is. So, big businesses don't create jobs, big businesses buy jobs. They buy smaller businesses. The small business is the one that generates the wealth that creates the product that has the hope for the future. And let me emphasize who you are. You are the people that understand what to do, are educating yourselves how to do it better, and have committed yourself to helping others accomplish that as well. That is not only good for you and good for your family, but good for the nation and good for the future. So in the course of what you are doing, don't ever, ever be discouraged, because you are the ones that make it work.

Now in the course of doing that let me say that there are those who will discourage you. There are those that will tell you that you can't do it. Or there are those that lose faith. George Washington said, "Nothing of significance was ever accomplished in life without great sacrifice." In other words, it is essential for those to do something better. A person who keeps doing what they are doing can never progress. But a person who takes a weekend off to come and learn from people that have been successful and then commit themselves to helping others, there are struggles in that, but there is also a reward in it. As I said, not every time can everybody see it.

Winston Churchill was Lord of the Admiralty during World War I. And in the period between World War I and World War II, he was a fellow that had lots of ideas. And he wanted to do things. And there are people that were jealous of that, and there always have been and there always will be. And so the leaders of the government and Britain, all during the 1930s, they made decisions to not allow Winston Churchill in government anyplace. During that time, Hitler, who was prospering in Germany, was violating all of the treaties after World War I. He was building lots of tanks and building his Army, and Churchill was saying to the government in Britain, "You need to understand, he is not making those tanks for parades; he intends to use them in a war. You should watch out." And everybody said, "Oh, you are just a troublemaker. You don't understand. We've already gone through a war and you are just trying to stir up problems." And so they locked him out. Rather than being in government he sat down at his home. And there by the lake he had a little easel and he just sat there and painted for all those many years.

And people would come and visit him, and he was left out of it. Eventually, in 1936, Hitler began to make his moves. He went into one country, then in another, and then another, until finally by 1940 Hitler and their third Reich dominated all of Europe. Now, when people realized that Churchill had been right, they turned to him.

Now let me explain to you why I use this example. That is that in any country, the strength of a country is found in four things: 1) Economic power. That is the strength of its currency and its capacity to create jobs. 2) Military power; we understand what that is, defense. 3) Its political system. Do people believe in their political system? Or, as we saw in Egypt and in Tunisia, are they are rioting and tearing it down? But then, 4) is leadership. So, let's go back and look at that: economic, military, political and leadership.

Now during this time in the 1930s, Britain was the most powerful nation on earth, bar none. One person in four on the planet lived in the British Empire. It was considered the military power on the planet. It had the longest political system, but it lacked leadership, until finally by 1940 all of Europe had been lost and they turned to Winston Churchill. And Winston now became a head of a country where nothing had changed. Everything was the same as it was the day before, but they were ready to surrender. They were ready to give up. They realized that they had blown it, and they changed. All the change was in leadership. Winston got up to speak for the first time, and the country was very frightened as to what would happen. In fact, they had arranged a peace conference to meet with Hitler, because Britain they felt was finished, and the Prime Minister didn't want to surrender his country, and so he quit. And

Britain is now on the ropes. They couldn't have an election. They didn't have time for that. The King called up Winston and said, "Let's make you Prime Minister." So he then went to Parliament and he gave this speech. Let me just share a little bit with you. And understand, this is a nation that is flat on its back. It's left alone. And here is what he said:

> "The battle of France is over. I expect the battle of Britain to begin. Upon this battle depends the survival of all Christian civilization. Upon it depends our British life. The fury and might of the enemy will soon be turned upon us. Hitler knows that he has to break us on this island or lose the war. We can stand up to him, and if we can, all Europe will be freed, and the life of the world may move forward into sunlit Uplands. But if we flag or if we fail, what shall happen? Let me tell you what we shall do. We shall go on to the end, we shall fight in France. We shall fight on the seas. We shall fight on the oceans. We shall fight with growing confidence and growing strength in the air. We shall defend our island, whatever may be the cost. We shall fight on the beaches. We shall fight on the landing grounds. We shall fight in the fields and in the streets. We shall fight in the hills, but we shall never surrender. For if we fail, then the whole world, including the United States, including all that we have known and cared for will sink into abyss of darkness. Therefore, let us brace ourselves for our duties. And so bear ourselves that if the British Empire and its commonwealth lasts for 1,000 years, the people will say of its history, this was their finest hour."

What is the point? The point is that there was a nation. Here was a nation that had lost its way. It was a nation that needed leadership. And regardless of the size of its army it was losing. Regardless of its great political history it was losing. Regardless of the size of its economy, it was losing. Why, because it didn't have leadership. Leadership requires integrity. It requires principle. It requires someone who is solid and who has a standard of right and wrong and has the personal responsibility to lead. Now when that person does that, they come under attack. And that is why they either float into oblivion or they make a change for all time.

The people that we honor are the people that chose to do something. In 1776, during the time that George Washington was at Valley Forge, he had started out with 40,000 soldiers at the beginning of the year. By the middle of the summer it was down to 25,000. And here he was in this encampment with 7,500 of whom only 2,500 could get up and walk. They didn't have boots, because the leather was so flimsy that it froze and cracked, and so what they had done was taken burlap and wrapped them around their feet. And he said, "We are going to attack, because if we don't we shall not have a nation." And so he had a password; the password was "Victory or Death." And on Christmas Eve 5,000 of them couldn't even march, couldn't even move. He got the 2,500 that could move, and he got up and he marched across the Delaware River, attacked the German Haitian soldiers that were there, and they had the first victory of the Revolution that then began the birth of a nation. He was one man, one person. Had he not done that, there would have been no United States of America. Had Winston Churchill not been able to rally his country, World War II would have never happened. The United States didn't get into the war for two more years. Had they surrendered and Hitler taken over all of Britain as well, there would have been no nation as we have seen.

What you have and what we are fighting is an economic war. There are those who want to say to you, you can't do something. There are those who are more dangerous. If you do step out and do something, they want the reward and take it away from you to discourage you from doing it. Where do you fit in? You fit in, in a unique time in which you have the skills, the experience and the mentorship in order to build an opportunity for yourselves and your family so that you need not fear the future. Then ten or twenty years from now, your grandchildren will have a framed picture of you on their fireplace and they will say, "There's where my grandpa decided that he was going to go the extra mile. He was going to pay the price. He was going to work harder. He was going to help more people. He was going to bless more folks. He created an opportunity that has now cascaded down to us through the years."

When people stand on this stage, they will look to that person as someone who paid the price and did it. I repeat, that is not only beneficial for you. Mr. Carrier made his air-conditioner so that we could stand here and be more comfortable. That is the byproduct of what he did. What you are doing is giving hope, giving leadership, giving integrity so that in the years to come others will rise up, as the scripture says, and call you blessed. God bless. Thank you.

———————

# CHAPTER 10 – THE CONSEQUENCES OF A NON-MORAL SOCIETY by Neil Mammen

There's a tendency amongst some folks to make declarations that sound good but are completely false. One of these is the declaration that "You can't legislate morality!"

I always find this to be amusing. If anyone states this to you, ask them this, "Why do you think that? Can you show me one law that is not based on a moral value?"

If they have trouble (which they will) suggest the laws against murder or stealing. Oh wait; those *are* based on moral values. How about the law against rape or incest? OK that doesn't work either as both of those are based on moral values too. You can keep playing with them till they give up. Then say: Look, let's be frank, nobody legislates anything **but** moral values.

Now it's true that sometimes those moral values will not be *your* moral values, but it will be someone's.

Another declaration you may hear is "It's wrong to force your moral values on other people!" But this is just as silly a complaint as the last one. To refute this merely say: "Excuse me, isn't that your moral value? Then why are you suggesting that it be imposed on other people?"

All laws legislate someone's moral values and all laws impose those moral values on other people, some who may not agree with the law. There's no way around it. The question really is should we legislate Mother Teresa's moral values or Hitler's?

I suggest that we don't legislate either, we should legislate objective moral laws that are transcendent and unchanging.

But are there transcendent unchanging objective moral laws? And if there are, where do they come from? How do we recognize them? If they apply to all mankind, then they can't come from a majority vote (otherwise slavery would have been moral in the 1800's when over 50% of the population agreed with it), nor can they come from a dictatorial leader (because who gave him the authority to make moral laws), nor can they come from some arbitrary decision by a committee. They can only come from someone who has authority over all mankind, someone who is in charge of all mankind. Well, who could that be? I suggest that could only be the Creator of mankind, i.e. God. And though out of the scope of this book, we can also prove that God's laws are all objective and not based on any capricious whim of His, but in fact based on His objective nature[1].

Previously we asked: Do we legislate Mother Teresa's moral values or Hitler's moral values? We can now conclude that the correct answer is that we should legislate the laws of the Creator of the Universe. The Creator of Nature, the Creator of Man. Those laws are also known as the "Natural Laws" or "The Laws of Nature and Nature's God.

---

1    See Is God Capricious, "Jesus Is Involved In Politics! Why aren't you? Why isn't your church?" Neil Mammen, Rational Free Press 2010

## The Laws of Nature and [the Laws] of Nature's God: What are these laws? How did we get them?

To the founding fathers and all Christians these laws come from God and all our laws must be subservient and based on these primary laws. But how do we know what these laws are? Well, *our knowledge* of these laws can come from three sources.

1. The Revealed Laws: To protect us from pain (and show us the path to Salvation), God supernaturally revealed many of the laws through the Bible. We believe these revealed laws are far superior and fuller than the next two sources.
2. The Conscience Laws: Other laws are written in our conscience. We *all* have them, though over time we can learn to harden our hearts to some of them. We also refer to these laws as the Self-Evident Laws. See Romans 2:14-15.[2]
3. The Moral Laws of Nature, the Discovered Laws: The third set of laws, are laws that we can logically derive just from nature. And if you think about that, it makes sense. After all, if God exists, He would have created an orderly universe based on a system of laws, laws that we believe are part of His very Character. If we study Creation we'll learn how it works. Just like the natural laws of physics.

Let's look at that last set, the Discovered Laws (or the Discoverable Laws). As mentioned, in this last group,

2   Romans 2: 14 Indeed, when Gentiles, who do not have the law, do by nature things required by the law, they are a law for themselves, even though they do not have the law, 15 since they show that the requirements of the law are written on their hearts, their consciences also bearing witness, and their thoughts now accusing, now even defending them.

are the laws, that even if we didn't learn them from God, we could eventually figure them out by rational thought. Even before Christ, men like Cicero (a contemporary of Julius Caesar), figured out that there *was* a Natural Law and it was ordained by *the* Supreme God *or* gods (Cicero just didn't know *which* God that was). Cicero realized that if you keep evaluating what prevented pain and worked and what caused pain and thus *didn't* work, you'd eventually be able to come up with an objective rational system of moral laws. They wouldn't be complete, but they could each be valid. Moral laws are what keep us safe, they are the instructions for reducing pain. These Discoverable Laws were also called "The Natural Law." Obeying the Natural Law would allow any civilization to advance rapidly, be the most productive, and reduce the causes of pain and suffering. When we violate these laws, our society learns from the "school of hard knocks" what they are and why those laws exist.[3] Note too that when we violate the Revealed Laws, we may rediscover some of them as Discovered Laws.

**Why were laws given to us?**

Some people think laws were made to oppress and control us. But let's think this through. What's the intent behind a senator or representative in congress writing a law that says all children must ride in a child car seat? Why are speed limit laws enacted?

Well, obviously in these cases laws are made to protect people. Car seats protect babies in case of a sudden stop or an accident. Speed limits protect

---

3   Sadly for Cicero, Mark Anthony found Cicero's moral concerns to be dangerous to men with ambitions of supreme power, and had him assassinated.

pedestrians and drivers. Contract laws protect both parties who make an agreement. Now notice, if an individual violates a traffic law, he not only could harm himself, but he could also harm other people, (generally if a person does something that could only harm himself with no chance of harming others we tend not to legislate overly against it.)

So if our legislature makes laws to protect us, why did God give us His moral laws? Obviously for the same reason, to protect us as well. So if an individual disobeys God's moral laws, he could harm himself or others. If he harms others then it behooves even a secular society to make laws against that action. And if that society does not make laws against that, over time they will come face to face with the discovered law, i.e. the horrible consequences of disobeying the laws of Nature and of Nature's God. So a "good" society will eventually legislate their nation's laws to reflect God's moral laws.

So what are the consequences of a non-moral society? Well, obviously it's pain and suffering. And note that when pain and suffering occurs it will first occur to the poor and the weak, to the widow and the orphan. Rich people can usually avoid the effects of bad laws for longer than the poor.

Now given all that, it's very easy for us to say well obviously we should have laws against stealing or murder or rape or cheating. What about the other non-obvious laws. What happens if a culture says we should not worry about sexual morals as they are old fashioned and out dated. Were those moral laws put in place for a reason? Let's now take a look at some of the consequences of these.

## Divorce

In the Bible, Jesus said that God hates divorce and recommended that we discourage it. Our forefathers agreed and their laws made divorce tough. Yet the secular world suggested that divorce is good for women and children. They asked: Why force children to live in a house where parents hate each other? And why force women to stay in an unhappy marriage?

So under pressure from the secularists, these laws were changed in 1969 and through the 70's. Prior to that people needed good reasons for divorce. Now you can get a divorce for any reason you want.

Forty years later we've found out why God said divorce was bad. Though only 30% of all US kids come from broken homes, it turns out that these unfortunate victims of divorce and single parent families account for over 70% of our prison population, 60% of rapists, 75% of adolescents charged with murder, 80% of those classified as motivated by displaced anger.[4] These unfortunate kids also are four times more likely to fail in school, have a 10-15% higher delinquency, three times more likely to attempt suicide, and young girls in this demographic are more sexually active at earlier ages. Broken homes also constitute most of our welfare cases.

In addition studies have shown women who are divorced rather than being better off are sicker and poorer[5] and sadder[6].

---

4    These and subsequent facts from: http://family.custhelp.com/cgi-bin/family.cfg/php/enduser/std_adp.php?p_faqid=1161

5    Divorce makes women sick, The Week page 22, Nov 17, 2006 Issue 285

6    Linda J. Waite, Don Browning, William J. Doherty, Maggie Gallagher, Ye Luo, and Scott M. Stanley http://deltabravo.net/custody/marriagestudy.php

There is a reason why God hates divorce, it's because it causes pain and suffering. Surely we can see the consequences of a non-moral society?

## Same-Sex marriage, Polygamy and Polyandry

Same-Sex Marriage (SSM) is promoted as an equalizer and we are asked to support it like we'd support inter-racial marriage. Marriage they claim is all about love. But SSM is not an equalizer, for homosexual couples even when "married" are rarely ever monogamous. In fact even studies by homosexual psychologists have indicated that monogamy is hardly[7] ever practiced. Secondly numerous studies have shown that children need a father and a mother, and a lack of one or the other results in statistics similar to broken homes. Thus any SSM union that adopts kids would deprive them of one parent and put them at risk.[8]

Polygamy (multiple wives) is a natural extension of same-sex marriage. If marriage is about love then why limit it to two people. Surely, we can love more than one person. Yet, there are severe consequences to polygamy. If just one tenth of the men in America were to marry three wives, there would be a 20% short-age of women for men to marry. This imbalance would severely destabilize our culture. In fact, as we've seen in polygamous societies of the past, young males who cannot find or fail to successfully compete for wives become a threat to the dominant males and usually

7   "Fidelity is not defined in terms of sexual behavior, but rather by their emotional commitment to one another" (The Male Couple; David P. McWhirter, M.D., and Andrew M. Mattison, M.S.W., Ph.D.; Prentice-Hall, 1984; p 252). The researchers were a gay couple and found 2/3rd of their subjects started monoga-mous but shortly later stopped being monogamous. Imagine if tomorrow we found out that over 65% of all married couples had not only cheated on each other but were now OK with that practice.

8   *Two Mommies Is One Too Many*, James C. Dobson, Time Magazine, Tuesday, Dec. 12, 2006

end up being kicked out of the community or if that is not possible (if the entire culture practices polygamy) they end up in roving gangs of rogue males. Polygamy could destroy the United States if it became legal and even a minority of the population started to practice it.[9]

Polyandry (multiple husbands) on the other hand has been shown to have significant problems.[10] It is embraced by very few men and women (less than 1%) and thus would not serve to balance the incidence of polygamy, even if both were instituted. Homosexuals, despite claims of their being 10% of the population are actually less than 2%,[11] so they would also not be sufficient to counter polygamy.[12]

## Cohabitation - living together before, or instead of, getting married

As most people now know, statistics[13] show that people who live together before marriage, rather than ensuring a strong marriage, actually have an increased chance of divorce.[14] But there are numerous other problems.

1. According to a Penn State study in 2000, married couples who lived together before they got mar-

9    Some authors have argued that the resulting excess of unmarried men requires leaders to wage wars to manage this population either by the capture of new women or the death of young men.

10    A study of polyandry in Tibetan cultures shows that it has significant problems and has been unappealing to most independent males. It most often is practiced in Tibet by brothers who share a wife and is usually done in an effort to keep the family farm intact without division. www.case.edu/affil/tibet/booksAndPapers/family.html?nw_view=1310368380&

11    www.traditionalvalues.org/pdf_files/UrbanLegend10percentMyth.pdf

12    2% gay + 1% polyandrous, removes only 3% of the males from needing mates. Compared to the 20% caused by polygamy. Remember you can't multiply the gays by 2 because they'd be marrying *each other*.

13    Except were noted, information taken from www.citizenlink.org/FOSI/marriage/cohabitation/A000000888.cfm last visited 4/25/07.

14    Cohabitation and Marital Stability: Quality or Commitment? Elizabeth Thomson, Ugo Colella. Journal of Marriage and the Family, Vol. 54, No. 2 (May, 1992), pp. 259-267 doi:10.2307/353057

ried show poorer communication skills than those who didn't live together first.[15]

2. Cohabiters have a higher incidence of violence and abuse than married people.
3. The National Institute of Mental Health (NIMH) found that women in cohabiting relationships had rates of depression nearly **five times higher** than married women, second only to women who were twice divorced.
4. The National Sex Survey reports that cohabiting men are nearly **four times more** likely than husbands to cheat on their partner in the past year, and while women are generally more faithful than men, cohabiting women are **eight times more** likely than wives to cheat.[16]
5. The National Marriage Project reports that while the poverty rate for children living in married households is about **6%**, it is **31%** for children in cohabiting homes, and closer to the **45%** for children living in single parent families.

When children are born into this relationship as they invariably are, we get more broken homes, more messed up kids, more messed up and depressed women, more welfare, more crime, and more divorce. The vicious cycle repeats.

Cohabitation is a simply a stupid, mean & incredibly selfish idea when you look at the statistics. Why would anyone want to set themselves and their future kids up for pain? Yes, I know that you may know one or two cohabitators that have stayed together, but we also

---

15   www.psu.edu/ur/2000/co-habit.html last visited 4/28/07
16   Naturally, the word "cheating" indicates that the partners had agreed to be monogamous and one wasn't.

know a few 95 year old smokers. Why does this statistical deviation not convince you that smoking is beneficial and should be promoted by government and the media? Any law or policy that encourages cohabitation, like health benefits for partners, easier adoption laws outside of marriage, tax deductions for cohabiters and so on will encourage and increase its incidence and hurt the innocent.

## Who will protect the innocent?

Any claim for "equal" rights is selfish and indicates these folks don't care about kids or facts, only about their own desires. Societies must not reward behavior that will damage its very own foundation. But who will pass those laws? Not liberals. Not non-Christians. Do you really think we have no responsibility here? Should not this be preached in sermons in every church? Why is it not happening? And is just preaching sermons enough? Should we not act to change the cause of the pain? Change the law that encourages this behavior.

My question to Christians is simply this: How can we say we love our neighbors if we let our government legislate laws that will hurt children? How can we say we love our neighbors if we let our government consist of men and women who would legislate laws that violate God's moral laws and thus bring death and destruction to future generations? Who will stand in the gap? Who loves enough to work to make a change in our nation's laws? Will it be you?

---

# CHAPTER 11 - WHAT CAN I DO

I know you can do more than you think!!! It's so easy not to get involved, because our lives are so full already. Also there may be a lack of interest or belief that you can make a difference. Well you can! It is extremely important to be concerned with leaders we have in the White House and other branches of government. It is vital that Christians get involved in the electoral process to save the Biblical principles we have discussed in this book. You can be the seed that gives birth to people who are only accessible to your influence.

One person of influence in my life is Richard M. DeVos (who likes to be called Rich). He is the co-founder of the Alticor Corporation. Because of my parents business success and relationship with Rich and Helen DeVos, Sharon and I along with my brother Frank Jr. and his wife Barbara were invited to join Mom & Dad and the DeVos's on their yacht Enterprise in Nantucket, MA for a week. Sharon and I were only married for two years and I was still in college. One of my classes was Psychology. At the time, my college professor was a single, good looking 28 year old and was teaching on situational ethics. It was 1970 when mini-skirts were the fashion and she liked to write on the chalk board (for a young man this can be very dangerous).

During that week on the yacht, I had a chance to visit with Rich one-on-one and I was explaining what the professor was teaching us about ethics. Rich stopped me in my tracks and said something like "young man, let me give you some important advice. No matter what time, place or situation, if what you are being taught disagrees with the Bible you would be very wise not to follow those instructions." Rich was someone I admired and respected from the time I was 13 years old. He used to do business meetings in my parent's garage. It was because of his influence that I started reading my Bible and grasped a greater understanding of what God's message meant to me. I praise God for my parent's success that lead to that relationship with Rich. It paved a way for me to change my life and the lives of my future generations forever. America needs more people like Rich who are willing to take the time to educate someone that is heading in the wrong direction. Calling the Called can help you to use your influence at the right time, place and situation to change someone's life around too! You will find that the right time, place and situation will actually be anytime the opportunity presents itself.

Two of my living heroes are Dexter & Birdie Yager. Years ago this couple started what is called *market place ministry* today. For the past thirty years this couple has used their Godly wisdom for building the most successful marketing business in the country, and it continues to this day. They also share their spiritual beliefs by offering a voluntary Christian church service at their major functions. As their business grows internationally, they offer the same option at their events, even in countries that it is not readily accepted. They have successfully transferred the leadership not only of their business, but the love of Christ so that their sons Doyle, Jeff and Steve are continuing their dream to many parts of the world." Through their Sunday morning services they have led hundreds of thousands of people to become believers in Jesus Christ and have made a major difference in their lives. They are a tremendous example of how you can use the place that God has positioned you to advance the kingdom. Offering an optional Christian service also helps countries, especially ours, to follow Christian principles and not elect people who violate those principles. The Bible is very clear on all subjects to have a happy fulfilled life. Those who don't believe that will one day discover their error. I realize that Dexter & Birdie Yager are a tremendous example to follow and many of us are not in that type of position of influence or choose to be there, however, we did choose to be where we are currently. That is important because God can use us right where we are. One person of influence can make a big difference no matter what platform they are on. Believe it or not, one vote has made significant differences throughout the history of our nation. These are just a few examples where one vote made the difference.

In the 1800 election Thomas Jefferson became President of the United States by one vote in the House of Representatives. Because of no majority in the electoral college by any candidate, the election was decided by the House.

The states of Washington, California, Texas and Oregon were voted into the U.S. by one vote.

President Andrew Johnson, like President Bill Clinton, was impeached by the House of Representatives. Both of them were voted not to be removed from office by the Senate. In Johnson's case, it was by only one vote.

In 1948 at the Texas Convention, Lynden B Johnson got one more vote then Coke Stevens and became the U.S. Senator for Texas.

In 1993 Al Gore became the deciding vote in the Senate to pass the increase in Social Security. Payments were to be 85% taxable, which was up from 50%.

I know being active has its risks. However, for Christians not to be active in our country right now will have grave results. The blood and treasure of our Christian Forefathers that fought and died to form this nation on Godly principles paid a much greater price then you or I will ever have to pay. We have to watch closely the way our government is being directed today by Progressive Politician's. A Progressive Politician is any person that wants greater government expansion, control over our lives (liberty), and control over the tools of production (control over businesses). A person can be a Progressive no matter what party label they carry. They tend to be elitists. They think that a few people with educated knowledge can run the country better than the voice of its citizens through voting. Common sense is not so common to these types of people. Their goal would be to divide and conquer by pointing out our differences: race, income level, education and faith. This process is used by dictators when they want to take over a country and we should be aware of it and stop it.

America is the melting pot of the world and allows anyone the opportunity to better themselves by making sacrifices and personal growth. You must have a free economy to allow people to succeed or fail and the opportunity to grow through both their successes and their failures. The United States is not perfect. We have made mistakes and by the grace of God we were given the opportunity to correct them. We can avoid suffering for ourselves and for others if we help society follow God's plan for life. You would have never read this far in this book if there was not the spark in you to know that our country needs to change the direction its going. You know in your spirit that you are "called" so don't let fear, laziness or excuses stop you from your calling to do your part. The pain of growth and stepping out of your comfort zone is so much less than the pain of regret! We must do our best to elect people who are not afraid to stand up for Christian principles that are the basis of our Constitution. No one forces anyone to become a Christian. That is a personal choice. However, nations that follow these principles have proven to be better for their citizens.

What can you do? Here are a few suggestions:

The first step in anything you do is pray. Pray for courage, pray for conviction, pray for wisdom, pray for understanding and most of all pray for forgiveness for those who just don't understand and don't take the threat to our country seriously. It is said that fifteen to twenty percent of the people in the colonies took up the challenge for freedom and changed the world. We don't need everyone, just those who are willing to make a difference.

Seek out information. In the references at the end of this book, I give you web sites of organizations and resource materials that you can look up and educate yourself. Don't try to be an expert before you venture out. Let your conviction and heart lead the way and the knowledge will come. Also give them a copy of this book.

Join activities that give you a platform to share what God has put on your heart. Run for local school boards, city council, planning committee's etc. If you don't run, find a candidate that you believe in and do all you can physically and financially to help him or her get elected. You can walk precincts, pass out flyers and contribute to the campaign.

Form a small group to meet at your home for a historical study of the Christian contributions which helped to develop our country. WWW.WALLBUILDERS.COM is a tremendous source for DVD's to watch and have a discussion about. Where areas of interest arise, set up assignments for the group for the next week's session.

Ask your Pastor if you can set up a small group at the church for researching candidates and/or issues for the upcoming election. This can be part of a prayer group that prays for our leaders.

Join your cities next leadership class. This will help you meet other leaders in your community and learn a lot about your city.

Get active in your Church. Learn what your Pastor, Elders & Deacons are doing and supporting in your church. Sometimes church leaders don't want the church to be *political*. Is there a difference in pushing for zone changes, building permits and upholding Godly principles in our elected leaders? The church at many times is going to be political anyway. So looking back at our country's history, it's time for the church and its leaders to be the leaders in the community again.

Help people to understand that the Constitution is the law of our land. We don't need to know what Shia law says and we don't need to know what is recommended in European countries. Our elected politicians and judges take an oath to protect and defend the Constitution of the United States. So when you hear any of these people talk about any other source then the Constitution, you should know it's time to get them out of office.

In conclusion I want to thank you for getting out of your comfort zone and becoming a person of influence. I know it can be difficult. However, knowing and trusting that God will provide what you need is a major blessing. I don't know of anyone that God used in the Bible that would say "that was easy". New friends will emerge, a new excitement will enter your life and most of all you will gain such an appreciation for the Christian Heritage of our country and the survival of these principles for future generations. I'll close with one of my hero's farewell message to the American people in November of 1994 when he was announcing his departure from political public life. Ronald Reagan said: "When the Lord calls me home, I will go with the greatest love for this country of ours and an eternal optimism for its future. I now begin the journey that will lead me into the sunset of my life. I know that for America, there will always be a bright dawn ahead."

My prayer and goal is that each generation can have that same kind of love for America and the Godly principles that formed this great nation. God bless you and remember that **"Jesus is the Answer."**

Sincerely, **Dennis P. Delisle**

**Bible verses to give you strength, guidance and application from Rhemarx: www.clingtoyourconfession.com.**

I have the mind of Christ – 1 Corinthians 2:16

I am highly favored in the sight of God and Man – Proverbs 3:4

I have authority over all the power of the enemy – Luke 10:19

The favor of God is producing great victories in the mist of great impossibilities – Joshua 11:20

I have favor and good understanding in the sight of God and Man – Proverbs 3:4

God is able to do exceedingly abundantly above all I could imagine – Ephesians 3:20

Send forth laborers into His harvest – Matthew 9:38

Therefore, we say with our mouth and believe in our heart – Romans 10:8-9

Every knee will bow and every tongue confess, Jesus is Lord in this city, _____, this county_____, this state_____ and our country of the United States of America), in Jesus name - Philippians 2:10

 CALLING THE CALLED

## CHAPTER 12 - RESOURCES

➤ WWW.CLINGTOYOURCONFESSION.COM – Positive confessions from the Word for daily inspiration.

➤ WWW.WALLBUILDERS.COM – Presenting America's forgotten history and hero's with an emphasis on our moral, religious, and constitutional heritage.

➤ WWW.NOBLINDFAITH.COM – A voice for apologetics. A discipline of defending a position (often religious) through systematic use if reason.

➤ WWW.VAC.ORG – Values Advocacy Council. VAC was formed to be a voice for Judeo-Christian Values in public matter.

➤ WWW.CHAMPIONTHEVOTE.COM – Website to help Christians on how they can help register 5 million new Christian voters.

➤ WWW.VOTEYOURFAITH.COM – Biblical principles at the ballot box.

➤ WWW.LEARNOURHISTORY.COM – Helping kids learn and have fun with history. It is designed to teach our children historical facts without bias.

➤ WWW.TRADITIONALVALUES.ORG – An inter-denominational public policy organization speaking on behalf of over 43,000 churches.

> WWW.FRC.ORG – The Family Research Council was created to advance faith, family and freedom in public policies and opinion. Through outreach to pastors they help equip churches to transform cultures.

> WWW.PJI.ORG – Pacific Justice Institute – A legal defense organization specializing in the defense of religious freedom, parent's rights and other civic liberties all without charge to provide clients with legal support they need.

> WWW.ACLJ.ORG – American Center for Law & Justice – focuses on constitutional law and human rights. A pro-life organization that is dedicated to the ideals that freedom of religion and that freedom of speech is an inalienable God given right for all people.

> WWW.FOCUSONTHEFAMILY.COM – Helping families thrive. Christian ministry to provide help and resources to couples to build healthy marriages that reflect Gods design and for parents to raise their children according to moral and values grounded in biblical principles.

> WWW.MORALLAW.ORG – Defending our inalienable right to biblically acknowledge God. Judge Roy S. Moore

> WWW.TRUTHINACTION.ORG. – Dr. James Kennedy – a media ministry that educates, motivates and activates believers to see the world in light of God's truth and transform their culture for Christ.

> WWW.PRINCIPLESTUDIES.ORG – Biblical principles of government. Is a research and educational founded

as a Christian alternative to many well established secular think tanks,

➢ WWW.SS.CA.GOV/ELECTIONS/VRDIS.PDF. – For voters registration form for CA. Voter's registration cards are available from a number of sources, including your County Registrar of Voters and Department of Motor Vehicles. There are internet sites and many states you can go directly to the Secretary of State's Office.

➢ WWW.NCCS.NET – National Center for Constitutional Studies.

➢ WWW.SUMMIT.ORG – Summit Ministries is an educational Christian Ministry whose very existence is a response to our current post-Christian culture.

➢ WWW.PATRIOTPOST.US – This site is highly acclaimed advocate of essential liberty and the restoration of the Constitutional limits of government.

➢ WWW.TOTALTRUTHBOOK.COM – Nancy Pearcey goal to liberate Christians from the cultural captivity.

➢ WWW.RESTORINGTHEPOWER.COM – Restoring the godly wisdom and knowledge that brought liberty to our nation.

➢ WWW.ALLIANCEDEFENSEFUND.ORG – ADF is a legal alliance defending the right to hear and speak the truth through strategy, funding and direct litigation.

➢ WWW.LC.ORG – Liberty Counsel is an international non-profit litigation, education and policy organization dedicated to advancing religious freedom. Matthew D. Staver, Esq.

- WWW.CCGACTION.ORG – Catholic Lay apostolates for the common good.

- WWW.RONBALLTODAY.COM - Contributor to "Calling the Called". Learn more about Ron's Ministries on line.

- WWW.BOBMCEWEN.COM – Contributor to "Calling the Called". Bob McEwen is one of the greatest resources of God & Government available today.

- WWW.NRB.ORG – National Religious Broadcasters is dedicated to preserving our freedoms.

- WWW.HSLDA.ORG – The Home School Legal Defense Association works to preserve the freedoms necessary for those who intend to have their children taught at home. It also updates on the latest home schooling news.

- WWW.CATHOLICVOTE.ORG – Issues affecting the Catholic faith.

- WWW.PRIESTSFORLIFE.ORG – Issues affecting Catholics

- WWW.BECKETFUND.ORG – Issues affecting all denominations

- WWW.THOMASMORE.ORG – Renowned as a national non-profit public interest law firm to restore and defend the Judeo-Christian heritage and moral values.

- WWW.FREEDOMWORKS.ORG – Works, recruits, educates, trains, and mobilizes millions of volunteer activists to fight for less government, lower taxes, and more freedom.

Made in the USA
Charleston, SC
01 December 2012